W9-AVT-298

Praise for Victor Boc's
HOW TO SOLVE ALL YOUR MONEY PROBLEMS FOREVER

"Thanks a billion for the most valuable information I have ever received in my entire lifetime—barring none! This is more than a dream come true."

Dr. Vince A. Beasler, Shreveport, Louisiana

"It works!!! I have over $150,000 more than I had when I first read your book, and great potential for more."

Sarah Romanow, Longview, Texas

"I put your material into practice for the past month. All I can say is I am amazed. If only I could have gotten this twenty years ago, I could have spent them playing instead of struggling for a living. There is no way I can repay you for what you have done for me. Thanks for THE MILLION."

Jim Radcliff, Portland, Oregon

"This is the most fantastic and truthful information I have ever read. After the Bible, this should be #1 to read."

Robert Gagne, Plantsville, Connecticut

"What a remarkable secret! You really let the cat out of the bag with this one. I never would have thought of doing this if you had not told me about it.

Patty Anson, Toronto, Ontario, Canada

"This book will easily be worth millions of dollars to anyone that reads it and uses it. I know it was for me."

G. Nelson Rodriguez, Philadelphia, Pennsylvania

"I cannot thank you enough for your excellent book. I got it on my 32nd birthday; what a wonderful present! It has had a terrific impact on my life!"

Marty Schirn, Iowa City, Iowa

"I've gone through tons of books, but none has ever hit home like your two-prong method. There are so many money books. The difference between yours and theirs is that yours works! I'm amazed at the things that have happened in only 13 days. I know this is only the beginning."

Linda Banta, Chicago, Illinois

"I got your book and I am ecstatic with joy (to say the least)! I would not part with this information for any amount of money."

Louis J. Culmo, Ansonia, Connecticut

"I read and applied the secrets in your book. Since I am the scientific type, I wanted to document the results. After $38,000 coming in, I decided your system works."

Bill Elgen, Sacramento, California

"Blessings to you for what you have written. I find this material invaluable. It gives me a step-by-step routine—definite, clear and to-the-point. I will never forget you."

Martin E. Breithaupt, Glendale, California

"I believe this is what a lot of people need to read. Maybe if enough of our population could get ahold of this material, our country could get back on its feet. The U.S. needs something at this time. The whole economy is at stake."

Carol Schneider, Libby, Montana

"I have been looking for this all my life, and I'm 55 now. This is the easiest, simplest thing to do I have ever read, and I've studied a lot. Thank you very much. You have changed my life."

Dean C. Scott, Oklahoma City, Oklahoma

"A whole new world has opened up for me. Believe me, I tingle with excitement. I'm going all the way with your proven method."

Maria A. Lembros, Owings Mills, Maryland

"I am so very well pleased with it, if you should try to buy it from me, I'd charge you much more than I paid. Really think it's the best I've ever read."

Pearl Norman, San Antonio, Texas

"You are doing a wholesome, beneficial service (a rare commodity today). Thank you for reestablishing our trust in mankind."

Cliff Rowland, Hurst, Texas

"Your book is the one that puts it all together. I have read many books. Most were money, time and effort wasted. Yours is the first one that I wouldn't want to miss under any circumstance. A check is enclosed. Please send another one. I never want to be without a copy."

Charles W. Garrett, Burlington, North Carolina

"On 9/21, I am on the Merv Griffin show. How did this happen? You made it happen. Am I reverently appreciative of your mind? You betcha!"

Jay Conrad Levinson, San Rafael, California

"The book and its methods work. I just secured $1,000,000. Thank you. My friends are baffled at the change in my life. I'm 44 now, and it's nice to be on the other side of the fence finally."

Leo J. Lorge, Camarillo, California

"Frankly, I feel like I have been converted—to humanity! This book belongs in the hands of every thinking adult in the country, because IT WORKS!"

Paul J. Thoennes, Bloomington, Illinois

"If only I had this book years ago. But let me say I lay regrets aside and move ahead at 78 years young. I feel I have everything to gain. I am enclosing money for another copy. When my daughter saw mine, well, what can I say—she needs one of her own. Am I grateful for the day I saw your book!"

Maria Bender, Sutton, Nebraska

"I've never been rich before, but now I'm on my way! It's great!"

Trisha E. Morgan, Orlando, Florida

"I feel like a blind man who was searching for the light and finally regained vision. What more can I say except thank you for a new life. Now it's my turn to be successful."

Mitchell B. Mays, D.C., Lodi, California

"First of all, God bless you for being you. Received your book some 30 days ago—and needless to say, I am overwhelmed."

Dennis A. Miller, El Cajon, California

"I got your book from a college professor who uses it in a class. You are right about good things coming so fast you better be ready. I was caught off guard. Now a half million dollars later, I can catch my breath and say, Praise the Lord for your book!"

Steven K. Wilson, Denver, Colorado

"I was pretty well off already, so I thought what do I need this book for? Boy was I wrong! Now looking back I see my life was a joke. Now my business is prospering, my wife is so happy she's hard to live with, and I am as peaceful as the lake we sail on."

Dr. L. Gordon Johnson, Springfield, Missouri

"This is very serious. Since the purchase of your book I am near to being a millionaire. My delight is beyond words."

Joseph deMadet, Miami, Florida

"There is no way I can thank you enough. Surely, we are brothers now, for I have received your counsel, and I have come to know your truth. As for your love, I am sure we are one in it."

Ronny Gullotta, Farmingdale, New York

"This is the most fantastic book I have ever read. I spent hundreds of dollars on money schemes that are absolutely useless. For the first time in my life I am free of money problems. If people would read this they could receive the same peace of mind that I have."

Mary Baker, Englewood, Ohio

"Your book did not leave my hands until it was completely read. For me, it was like finding the missing link. You have broken the code. You have found the key. I see now what I was missing. It is the key to attaining everything I ever wanted."

Joseph R. Ducote, Leonardtown, Maryland

"Well, you're hearing from me and you've probably heard from many others. I guess they all love you. I guess I love you too."

Lauren Ridge, East Setauket, New York

ALSO BY VICTOR BOC

Money Talks

The Business Income Generating Network

*Tamper: The Game of High-Impact Business
for Shrewd Investors*

Maximum Productivity System

The Electric Yellow Pages

Wordrace

Be Healthy—Beyond Your Wildest Dreams

Just Living and Reproducing

Georgia Bear Can't Dance

The Ranger

HOW TO
SOLVE
ALL YOUR
MONEY PROBLEMS
FOREVER

CREATING A POSITIVE FLOW OF MONEY INTO YOUR LIFE

VICTOR BOC

THIRD EDITION

Vorco
PUBLISHING

Eugene, Oregon

This book is intended to provide information regarding the subject covered. It is sold with the understanding that the author is not engaged in legal or professional services. If such services are desired, a competent professional should be sought. The purpose of this book is to inform and entertain. The author and publisher assume no liability, direct or indirect, resulting from the use or misuse of this information. In no case, regardless of the form of claim, shall liability exceed the cost of book replacement or refund. Anyone not wishing to agree to these terms may return this book to the publisher for a full refund.

VORCO PUBLISHING
P.O. Box 5316, Eugene, Oregon 97405
email: vorco@aol.com

Copyright © 1996 by Victor Boc

All rights reserved. No portion of this book may be reproduced or transmitted, in any form whatsoever, without express written permission from the publisher.

First edition 1978. Second edition 1980.

THE TWO-PRONG METHOD™ is a trademark of Victor Boc. Trademark protection applies to all referrences in this book.

ISBN: 0-912937-31-9
Library of Congress Catalog Card Number: 95-90816

Publisher's Cataloging in Publication

Boc, Victor
    How to solve all your money problems forever / Victor Boc
    p. cm.
    Includes bibliographical references and index.
    Preassigned LCCN: 95-90816.
    ISBN 0-912937-31-9

    1. Finance, Personal.   I. Title

HG179.B63 1996   332.024
                    QBI95-20589

Manufactured in the United States of America
10 9 8 7 6 5 4 3 2 1

This book is dedicated to
my son, Matthew,
who was born in its pages.

Acknowledgments

THE FOLLOWING PEOPLE have, in one way or another, influenced the content of this book and thus deserve acknowledgment: Tom Engle, Jim Leonard, Joe Karbo, Paul Vorisek, Ken Vorisek, Bill Toomey, Diane Borosky, Margie Montagne, Larry Fortener, Donna Maddux, Bob Higgins, Cyndee Haines, Roger Watson, Ron McKinney, Doyle Brunson, Bobby Baldwin, Mark O. Haroldson, Dick Bertram, Michele O'Leary, Steve Kline, Herbert Shelton, Dave Wallace, Karen Tracy, Bob Bolen and Shelly King. I also wish to express appreciation and gratitude to my editor, Jacqueline Malone, for her brilliant work on this manuscript. Finally, a special acknowledgment goes to the man at 6th & Euclid—who made me look up.

CONTENTS

NOTICE

THE METHOD IN THIS BOOK will unquestionably create a positive flow of money into your life, perhaps for the first time ever. Be prepared. When this flow starts, money may come so quickly and in such great abundance that, unless you are ready, a state of shock could result. Consider yourself forewarned.

PREFACE
To The Third Edition

THIS BOOK WAS FIRST published in 1978, a second edition in 1980. By 1990, it had sold 200,000 copies worldwide, most of them through direct marketing. No one has yet written a book anything like this one. To this day, it stands alone in its class.

In recent years, I've received a flurry of letters and inquiries. Some ask advice, some make suggestions, some share success stories. They all want to know one thing: when the next edition of the book is coming out. Well, the wait is over. Here it is—an all-new publication, ready for the 21st century.

In this edition, I have revised and expanded the entire text. Although the message in this book is timeless, the material needed updating. We live in a different world today than we did fifteen years ago. The government attacks the deficit; politicians fight over the budget; everyone talks fiscal responsibility—and all the while, people endure their slavery to money. This book is needed now, perhaps more than ever.

I release this edition, confident it will enrich the lives of people from all corners of society. This book has the potential to bring us together and to contribute to an enlightened social fabric.

This edition remains plain and uncomplicated. I invite you to read it and use it. Join many thousands of people from across our global community who have discovered financial peace of mind.

In the opening pages, I quote a small sampling of letters I've received over the years. Notice I do not quote famous people, magazine editors or professional book reviewers. I could, but I don't think you'd be interested. I don't want a bunch of important people saying the book is well-written and ahead of its time. I want regular people who followed these instructions to share their experience. This book was written for you, not for intellectuals and critical analysts. They have their books.

Fate has a way of touching lives. Regardless of how this book made its way into your hands, it is part of your world now. Whether you know it or not, this book represents a milestone in the history of your life. Someday you will celebrate this encounter with destiny.

Victor Boc
January, 1996

How to Solve All Your Money Problems Forever

"I have been poor and I have been rich. Rich is better."
Sophie Tucker

Introduction

YOU HOLD IN YOUR HANDS information that can change your life. The printing is nothing special to look at, but what these few pages have to say is monumental. This book is unlike any other that has ever been written. You are very wise to have purchased it.

The information contained herein could be the most important you ever gain. As of this moment, complete and permanent financial security is yours if you want it. No matter who you are, no matter what you've experienced, no matter what abilities you possess (or lack), you can now free yourself from money worries forever. If you follow these instructions, your dreams will come true.

I have something to tell you—a secret. What you do with this secret is up to you. If you ignore it, your life will continue as always. If you act on it, your life will change quickly and dramatically. Today will be the dawning of a new day for you, day one of your new life. You will enter into a new consciousness, one that is free

from worry. Never again will you need to concern yourself with money; you will have all you want, whenever
you want it. Does the prospect of financial freedom sound
attractive to you? Well, my friend, it is knocking at your
door as you read this.

I have something to teach you. Please read my words
with an open mind. Do not be negative due to what you
believed in the past. Put all your past conditioning aside
for now and read my words with a willingness to learn. I
know I can help you, even if you think you know more
about the subject than I do.

Everything I am about to tell you is the truth. But
don't take my word for it. Prove it yourself. I will not—
and *cannot*—prove anything to you. The burden of proof
rests with you alone. All I can do is present the facts.

What I have to tell you may sound preposterous. Your
first reaction may be, "Come on now, you've got to be
kidding." The idea may run contrary to the way you've
always thought. But I assure you, the method works. In
fact, it cannot fail. The method is as reliable as jumping
off a chair. If you stand on a chair and jump off, you will
land on the floor. I know this to be true. It is true for me,
and I can say with confidence, it is true for you. So, too,
the information I give you in this book must produce
the desired results. The method has worked for me, and
it will work for you—if you let it. Just give it a try, and
you will see.

Look at your life. Are you satisfied with your financial situation? Are you at peace with what you've accomplished so far? Are you happy with where you're headed?
If you are like most people, you have a nagging sense
that your life is somehow unfulfilled. You feel frustrated
and dissatisfied with attempts to quench your desires.

Henry David Thoreau said, "Most people lead lives of quiet desperation." That is true. And for most people, a huge part of their misery appears to revolve around money. They can't get enough of it, and when they do, they can't hang on to it. For the majority of people, money is an ugly, energy-draining worry. And the worry is always there, ever present. No matter what they try, nothing relieves this constant torment.

How about you? Do you ever worry about money? Do you worry about being able to meet expenses? Do you worry about the welfare of those who depend on you? Do you worry about how much money you will have five, ten, twenty years from now?

How would you like to eliminate all that wasted energy from your life? How would you like to end your slavery to the pursuit of money? How would you like to establish a strong and lasting flow of money into your life? Well, now you can.

Just imagine. Finally, you can devote your energy to worthy aspirations instead of to meaningless struggles. You can pursue projects and interests you've been meaning to tackle but never get around to. You can spend time with friends and family, and give needed attention to relationships. You can do whatever you want, whenever you want to do it. Worry about something else if you must, but you will no longer need to worry about money.

We hear a lot about stress these days; everyone understands its negative effects. But how can you reduce stress if you must constantly worry about money? How can you relax when your life is in disarray? Let me ask you: Do you want to fix your life? Do you want to pull your act together and get on track? If you do, make this book your first step.

In this book, I show you how to solve all your money problems forever. I introduce "the two-prong method" and explain the particulars. I do not give vague instructions that leave you hanging in the air and wondering what to do next; I present complete and specific details on exactly what to do and how to begin. And doing this method is easy—in fact, it's fun. Furthermore, you do not need to have any money set aside in order to start, not one penny! These are strong statements, I realize, but every word is true.

Please read the chapters of this book in the sequence written. Do not skip around and pick out sections that look interesting. The subject matter is arranged in the order best assimilated, with each part based on a familiarity of previous material. Make sure you absorb the contents in the order intended.

As you read and study these pages, remember three points and take comfort in them:

(1) You will never regret the time you spend reading and mastering what is contained in this book.

(2) The instructions are easy to understand and simple to follow.

(3) Positive results are a certainty.

Go ahead, get excited! You are beginning a new journey, a new phase of your life. Along the way, every aspect of your financial situation will improve. Start the celebration now, for at last you have found a way to solve all your money problems forever.

"Life is the only game in which the object of the game is to learn the rules."
Ashleigh Brilliant

1

Money

A FEW YEARS AGO, a team of researchers from Columbia University conducted an unusual study. Over a period of weeks, they stationed themselves in the lobbies of various New York City banks in order to observe the behavior of people as they entered the banks and went about their business. The team recorded data such as facial expressions, eye movements, body language and behavior patterns.

The results of this study show that the average person becomes extremely tense as soon as he or she steps into a bank. The moment an individual enters that mysterious place where money resides, the person becomes deadly serious.

The same researchers conducted their observations in numerous other settings also, looking for qualities like respect and attentiveness. Nowhere were these qualities more apparent than in a bank, particularly in the presence of large sums of money. No place else, not even in church, did people behave more soberly.

These findings show that the one situation in which people are most solemn is when they are dealing with money. Human beings consider money a very serious matter, almost to the point of worship.

Feeling the presence...

What is this thing that means so much to everyone? What is money? Normally, when people think of money, they do not focus on the raw concept of money, but on how to acquire it, how to spend it and how to hang on to it. Most people spend a great deal of time thinking about money without ever contemplating what it is.

Remove a dollar bill from your wallet. Look at it. Roll it between your fingers. Feel it. What do you see? What do you feel? Do you think the piece of paper you hold in your hand is the essence of money?

As you hold the dollar bill, what emotions come up for you? What do you think causes those feelings? What causes you to become solemn inside the walls of a banking institution? What causes your eyes to dilate at the sight of a paper dollar? Do you suppose the slip of paper, by itself, is responsible for your feelings about money?

Most people go through life believing that money is nothing more than paper and coin. They are mistaken. These objects are merely symbols that denote an arbitrary value. Paper and coin are inanimate objects that have no power of their own, other than the power we assign to them. What makes them special is the agreement we have with others. What gives the paper and coin value is what they stand for.

Do not confuse money with yen, pounds, deutschemarks or Federal Reserve Notes. Items of currency have no intrinsic value as food, clothing or shelter. At best, items of currency can be exchanged for things of value, provided you are in the right country.

If you see money only as currency, you miss a critical point. Money is not matter. Money is an idea, a concept, a communication. The paper notes and the metal coins are not money. They represent money, but they are not, themselves, money. Money is that which lies beneath these material objects. That remarkable mystery, whatever it is, is the true identity of money.

Pondering the mystery...

Money wears many faces. Different people perceive money in different ways. The following are some of the most common ways people think of money.

As Security. Money can be thought of as a layer of protection that separates you from a cruel, uncaring world. Without money, you are thrown to the wolves, cast into the pit where losers go. Without money, you have no ability to control your destiny or to ward off hardhearted people who would beat you down.

Conventional wisdom says that if you have a large bank balance and a stable career, you have security. You have a hedge. You have something you can depend on to battle unpleasant feelings like worry and loneliness. To a greater or lesser degree, you can control others and get them to do what you want them to do. Even your health is, to some extent, affected by your ability to purchase quality health care. With money, if something goes wrong, you have the funds to buy whatever is needed to fix the problem. Accountants, lawyers, doctors, therapists—they all take money. Viewed this way, money translates into security.

As a problem. Chances are, when you think of money, you think in terms of a problem. This causes you to worry. You worry about how to make more of it and how to keep from losing the amount you have. For most people, money thoughts are worrisome thoughts.

This viewpoint, although prevalent, is not accurate. Money, by its nature, is not problematic. Furthermore, treating money as a problem serves no purpose. Worrying about money causes you to create a negative, self-defeating belief system based on greed and scarcity. Not only is this perspective false, it is counterproductive. Defining money as a problem makes it one, and when you view money in a negative light, money becomes far more elusive. In and of itself, money is not a problem and never needs to be.

As power. In our society, people with money appear to command respect, loyalty and compliance. In other words, money means power. People with money carry an aura of independence: they can do what they want, when they want and with whom they want. Wealthy people have the power to buy anything they desire. A new washing machine? No problem. A better stereo system? Here's the check. A bigger house? Let's look for one tomorrow.

From this perspective, everything carries a price tag. Even friends, marriage and intimacy require some amount of money. Although love and companionship do not directly involve the exchange of cash, some minimal degree of financial well-being is necessary to put yourself in a situation where these things can occur. The person with money need not be concerned about a lack of buying power or a lack of people willing to tag along. The person with money commands the power to affect others.

As a promise. When you use money as a means of exchange, you makes an implicit agreement regarding the values and customs surrounding that money. The use of money depends on an understanding of how people act regarding money and a belief that they will continue to act in a similar manner in the future. In this sense, money is a promise—a promise to make good, a promise that there exists something of value to follow in the wake of the coin or paper.

When you accept a dollar bill from someone, you are accepting a promise. Since the piece of paper is of no practical use, you agree to take the paper on the condition that someone else will accept it from you when you decide to spend it. That's a promise. Since United States Federal Reserve Notes are no longer backed by gold, they carry value only due to unstated agreements. When you use these notes, you do so based on the promise that people will continue to use them in the future.

As energy. Money influences, to some extent, all interactions in our society. And money is not just something out there in the world, something that is separate from you. Money is intimately linked to who you are and what you do. Truth is, when you deal with money, you are dealing with energy. From this perspective, money can be thought of as a measure of your applied life-force.

You have only so much time to be alive and functioning as a member of society, only so many days and hours to be productive on earth. When you do whatever you do to earn money, you are trading a portion of your allotted time, your reserve of energy, for money. In this sense, money equates with energy. The amount of money you have reflects the amount of energy you have stockpiled in your corner.

These are a few of many ways to perceive the essence of money. These viewpoints are not absolute, nor are they necessarily right for you; you are free to think of money in whatever way you choose.

So, what is money? I leave it to you to answer that question for yourself. Pondering the mystery of money is like meditating on an unsolvable paradox: you may never answer the question, but you learn something in trying.

I will say this: money is an essence that is positive and constructive. Money is a glorious gift for human beings on planet Earth. Money is a joyful promise of wonders to come. Money is a useful and comforting blanket of security. Money is a grand and precious power. Money is a pure, clean, beneficial manifestation of energy. Money is wonderful—and well worth having.

Regardless of what money is, regardless of what you deem it to be, I know you want it. That is good. And when you finish reading this book, you will know how to get it.

2

The Flow of Money

THREE BLIND MEN WERE LOST in the desert. They had been wandering for days in hope of finding their way back to civilization. The prospects looked grim.

At last, they came upon a camel. The animal stood motionless as each man reached out and touched it.

The first man touched the camel's leg. "A small tree," he declared. According to him, they had just come upon a tree in the desert.

The second man touched the camel's tail. He drew back in horror. "A snake!" he exclaimed. He warned the others to watch out for a large snake with its head in the air, preparing to strike.

The third man raised his hand high and touched the camel's hump. "It's a mound of dirt," he announced. He assured the others they had nothing to fear from a hill of sand in the desert.

The three men stepped back and began to argue with one another.

"It's a snake, I tell you. I felt its skinny body."

25

"You're wrong. It is too thick and firm to be a snake. It's a tree."

"You're both mistaken. How could you guys be so far off? It's a mound of dirt."

After several minutes of heated discussion, one of the men shouted, "This is ridiculous. How is it that we differ so much in our opinions? We have no area of agreement whatsoever."

The men thought about this comment for a brief time. Then, one of them spoke up. "You know, that's not true," he said. "We do have one area of agreement, one thing we all agree on."

"And what is that?" the first man asked.

"Well, we all agree that we have found *something*. We may not agree on what it is, but at least we agree that it is something, right?"

Suddenly, the three men realized the foolishness of their bickering. They shared a quick embrace and a few kind words. Then, determined to settle the dispute, they approached the mysterious object again. This time, each man felt the animal from head to toe. They all agreed they had found a camel. With that, they climbed aboard and rode safely out of the desert, back to civilization.

Dealing with something...

Whatever money is, whatever you perceive it to be, the main point you must understand is this: *money is something*. Before we proceed with this discussion, you must concur with me on this point. You and I may not agree on everything, but we surely agree that money, whatever it is, is something.

The idea that money is something may not seem revolutionary to you, but few people realize this fact. I have asked many individuals point blank, "What do you think money is?"

The most common response: "I don't know."

I then ask, "Is it anything at all?"

The usual reply is something like, "Gee, I never thought about that before."

If I persist with the questioning, most people end up expressing the belief that money must be dollar bills. The majority of people never realize that anything exists beyond the physical currency.

"I never thought money was anything," a woman in her eighties once told me. "I guess maybe it really is something after all."

You bet it is! Make no mistake about it, money is something. The nature of money may be esoteric or metaphysical, but it is real. The essence of money may not be coin or paper, but no matter what it is, it does exist somewhere on some level.

Feel free to think of money as some sort of strange energy if you wish. Think of it as an unknowable power if you want. Say money is intangible. Say it is elusive. Say this whole subject is weird. That's okay. Whatever you believe money to be, you must certainly admit that it is *something*, that it exists at some level of reality. For our purposes here, you need not concern yourself with exactly what money is; you need only know that it is "something." I repeat: *money is something*.

Why am I making such a big deal out of the fact that money is something? I'll tell you why—and this is an important point. If money is something, and if money does exist as something, then it must be subject to the same laws of physics that all other "somethings" are subject to. Lo and behold, this is precisely the case.

Obeying the laws...

Physics is an exact science. The laws of physics apply unerringly to the wide range of matter, activities and situations found in our incredibly diverse universe. The laws that govern our physical world are irrefutable.

In 1687, Sir Isaac Newton published what have become known as Newton's Three Laws of Motion. These laws describe the effect that forces have on objects. In the domain of common, physical interactions, these laws have proven to be a reliable formula for understanding and predicting motion. Briefly stated, Newton's three laws are:

(1) A body remains at rest unless it is acted upon by an unopposed force.

(2) An unopposed force acting on a body causes the body to accelerate in the direction of the force.

(3) For every force there is an equal and opposite force.

If you're not a wizard at physics, don't worry; you don't have to be. I will explain, in simple terms, what these three laws mean and how they relate to the flow of money.

Let's say there is an object with a force acting on it in one direction and, at the same time, another force acting on it in the opposite direction. (This describes the situation for every object in the universe.) Now, if the strength of both forces is equal, the forces balance each other, and the object does not move. If, however, one force is greater than the other force, then the object moves in the direction of the stronger force. Simple, huh?

Now go fly a kite. Not literally, of course, but imagine for a moment you are flying a kite. As you can see from the figure below, two opposing forces act on the kite.

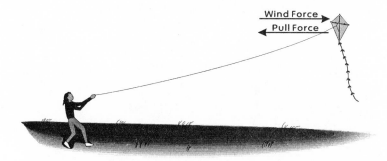

Wind Force
Pull Force

There is the force created by the wind against the kite. This force is pushing the kite away from you. At the same time, there is the force created by you pulling on the string. This force is pulling the kite toward you. So, there are two opposing forces, the wind force and the pull force.

If the two forces are equal, the kite remains a constant distance from you. This is what happens when you hold the kite in place. The force of the wind is trying to push the kite away from you, while, at the same time, you are pulling on the string with an equal and opposite force, trying to pull the kite toward you. When the two forces are equal, they balance each other, and the kite does not move in or out relative to you.

If you relax your hold, the string slides through your fingers. The force of the wind on the kite is then greater than the force of you pulling on the string, and the kite moves away from you. On the other hand, if you grip the string firmly and pull hard, your pull force is then greater than the wind force, and the kite moves toward you.

Flying a kite is an example of how opposing forces act on an object. This same principle applies to everything in the world. Any object, at any moment, has forces acting on it, even if you are unaware of those forces. The pen resting on your desk right now has opposing forces acting on it. If the pen is not moving, the lack of motion is not due to a lack of forces; the lack of motion is due to the fact that the forces that are acting on the pen are exactly equal and opposite. If an object is moving, the movement is due to a force that is not being opposed by a force of equal magnitude.

And so it is with money. Remember: *money is something*. So, if money exists, which it does, then money must also obey these same laws of physics. And it does.

We are not involved in some sort of a trick here. We are simply formulating a down-to-earth explanation of reality. These laws of physics must apply to money just as they apply to everything else in this world that is "something." Like every other thing there is, money does not exist in isolation; money, too, is constantly being acted upon by opposing forces.

Speaking of money...

The following figures illustrate how forces acting on money affect its flow. The figures show three important elements: *you*, *money*, and the *forces*. The forces are labeled *attractive force* (the force drawing money toward you) and *repellant force* (the force pushing money away from you). The length of each arrow represents the relative strength of each force. [Note: Although a drawing of a male is used in these figures, no slight to females is intended; everything in this book applies equally to men and women.]

In the first figure, your attractive force is equal to your repellant force. In this case, money neither moves toward you nor away from you. You are just getting by; every dime that comes in goes back out again.

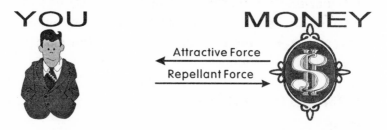

The next figure shows the situation when your repellant force is greater than your attractive force. Money flows away from you. Every day, you go deeper in debt.

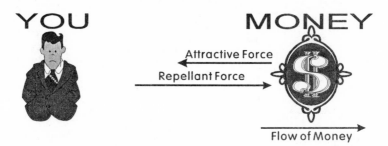

In the figure below, your attractive force is greater than your repellant force. Money flows in your direction. No matter what you do, you continue to get richer.

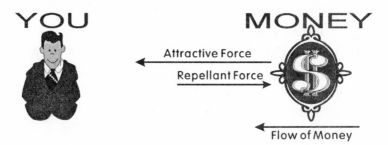

Realize that we are not speaking of money as a pile of dollar bills. We are referring to the essence of money. Realize, also, that although the forces acting on money are not forces in the purely physical sense, they are forces nonetheless. Once you realize that these forces exist and that you can control them, it becomes a simple matter for you to create and maintain a positive flow of money into your life.

Getting to the root...

Many factors contribute to attracting money to you, and many factors contribute to repelling money from you. In the following pages, you will learn exactly what attracts money and exactly what repels money.

Throughout this book, I speak of the "flow of money." This flow is of primary importance. If your attractive force is greater than your repellant force, money flows into your life. If your repellant force is greater than your attractive force, money flows out of your life.

Your objective is to increase the flow of money into your life. The *only* way money can flow into your life is if your attractive force is greater than your repellant force. What you need to do, therefore, is maximize your attractive force and, at the same time, minimize your repellant force. The method I describe in this book enables you to do these two things. It is called "the two-prong method."

The two-prong method consists of two separate techniques, one that will increase your attractive force and one that will decrease your repellant force. It acts directly on these two forces. No matter what your current financial situation, if you use the two-prong method, you will generate a positive flow of money into your life.

If you have difficulty obtaining and keeping money, then the flow of money is out of your life. In that case, your repellant force is greater than your attractive force. You need to reverse the relative strengths of the two forces. By increasing your attractive force and decreasing your repellant force, you create a positive flow of money for yourself.

Even if you are reasonably well off, even if you have no serious monetary problems at this time, you can still use the two-prong method to your benefit. The same strategy applies: maximize your attractive force and minimize your repellant force. This will result in an even greater flow of money in your direction.

No matter what your age, sex, appearance, handicaps, intelligence, or whatever, to break all barriers and create a massive flow of money into your life, you must do two things: maximize your attractive force and minimize your repellant force. The plan is simple. The results are certain.

What you need to do:

Maximize Your Attractive Force
Minimize Your Repellant Force

Keep in mind that, although these forces are abstract concepts, they represent the reality of all monetary situations. We are talking about the forces that govern the flow of money.

Granted, this is not the usual way people look at the issue of making money. But this approach is absolutely fundamental. In dealing with these forces, you are getting to the root of your monetary situation. There is no better place to start.

"As a man thinketh in his heart, so is he."

Proverbs 23:7

3

The Law
of Attraction

IN THE NEXT FOUR chapters, you will learn how to maximize the attractive force you radiate toward money. You will discover the Law of Attraction and learn a specific technique for attracting money into your life. If you apply this technique, you will transform everything you touch into an expression of prosperity.

A prosperous life involves many factors. Your income, your expenses, your debts and your money-management skills are all elements that affect your financial well-being. Every one of these elements functions in strict accordance with the Law of Attraction. Every situation you encounter in life is a testament to the power and reliability of this law.

The Law of Attraction is more far-reaching than most people imagine. Its ramifications are enormous. No circumstance lies beyond the forces commanded by the Law of Attraction. The application of this law can literally change your life—indeed, the entire world.

The Law of Attraction states: Maintaining any preconceived image of intelligence attracts the manifestation of that image in reality. In other words, the act of holding a particular image in your mind tends to materialize, in the real world, objects and situations that correspond to that image.

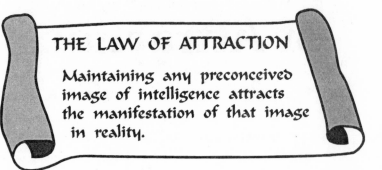

THE LAW OF ATTRACTION

Maintaining any preconceived image of intelligence attracts the manifestation of that image in reality.

First question: What is reality? When you think of reality, you probably think in terms of material objects, like the car in your garage, the table in your kitchen or the book in your hands. Most people believe reality exists somewhere "out there" in the external world.

Next question: What is imagination? When you think of imagination, you probably think in terms of visions, daydreams and private thoughts. Most people think imagination exists only in their mind.

Well, get ready for a surprise. Imagination and reality are intimately connected. What you commonly think of as reality is totally dependent on imagination.

REALITY IS THE DIRECT RESULT OF IMAGINATION.

The Law of Attraction means that when an image is implanted in your mind, unseen forces are set into motion, forces that seek to manifest that image in reality. A clear image implanted in your mind carries with it the power to attract whatever is necessary for complete manifestation.

Your mental images literally create your world. Whatever images you hold in your mind, those are the images that materialize. This fundamental concept underlies all reality and explains the development of your particular situation in life, be it favorable or unfavorable. In short, thoughts create reality.

Building bridges...

Every human-made object began its existence as an intangible bit of energy, an idea. Every invention ever invented, from the stone tablet to the cellular phone, began quietly as a thought in one person's mind.

Consider for a moment some inventions that have had a major impact on our lives:

Moveable type (1450). A printing press that allows type to be custom set for each printing.

Safety pin (1849). An item that allows for safe and easy fastening of articles.

Ballpoint pen (1888). A writing utensil that does not require dipping in an inkwell.

Zipper (1891). A way to open and close clothing by moving a sliding piece up and down.

Vacuum cleaner (1907). A machine to suck up dirt by passing over the area to be cleaned.

Electric toaster (1918). A device for easy toasting of individual slices of bread.

Radar (1922). A means of detecting objects at a distance regardless of lighting or conditions.

Television (1923). A technology that sends moving pictures through the air to a receiving box.

Talking movie (1927). A motion picture that contains synchronized sound right on the film.

Helicopter (1939). A flying vehicle that does not require horizontal motion to rise or land.

Transistor (1948). An electronic component to control current without the high voltage of tubes.

Video tape (1961). A technology for recording motion pictures on magnetic tape instead of film.

Personal computer (1975). A computer system small enough to fit on a desktop.

Roller blades (1979). Skates with in-line wheels for more efficient skating.

Fax machine (1980). A device to transfer printed material over the telephone line.

Compact disk (1983). A laser technology for digitally storing large amounts of music or data.

Liquid hand warmer (1988). A portable packet that requires no outside energy to generate heat.

Disposable contact lenses (1990). Inexpensive contacts that are discarded after wearing.

Caller ID (1993). A telephone service that displays who is calling before the phone is answered.

World Wide Web (1994). A means of linking information on the Internet using hypertext.

When you see a particular human achievement—the Golden Gate Bridge, for example—you are witnessing the physical expression of an idea that was born in one individual's creative imagination. The means of constructing the item (the financing, the materials, the project management and so forth) fall into place only after the image has been clearly visualized.

Any object you create begins its existence in the form of a concept. You cannot create anything unless it is first conceived in thought. After an image is planted in your mind—and only then—can plans go forward to bring about the realization of that image. That is why the first step of creation is the act of implanting an image.

The Law of Attraction says that when you fix in your mind the image of an object or circumstance, your image is, through whatever means necessary, attracted to you. In other words, you attract into your life whatever image you first hold in your mind.

> *"We are what we think. All that we are arises with our thoughts. And with our thoughts, we make our world."*
> The Buddha

Your life is a reflection of your thoughts. This idea is not a superstition. It is not even a matter of opinion. It is a well-established and demonstrable fact. Once you understand how your mind works, harnessing the creative power of the universe becomes child's play.

Working together...

Your mind has two components: your conscious mind and your subconscious mind. Each has unique capabilities and weaknesses.

Your conscious mind is the part of your mind you are aware of during waking hours. You use your conscious mind for cognitive thinking and logical reasoning. It is the faculty that processes information, the part of your mind where you evaluate problems and regulate voluntary activity.

Your conscious mind is the entity with which you make decisions. It selects what car to buy, what job to take, what friends to keep, what magazine to read and what dinner to order from the menu. With your conscious mind, you conduct rational thinking and weigh pros and cons to evaluate choices. In short, your conscious mind is responsible for all thinking of which you are consciously aware.

Your subconscious mind is quite different. Normally, you are unaware of your subconscious mind. This part of your mind lies hidden beneath conscious thinking.

Although you may be unaware of its functioning, your subconscious mind is always—repeat, always—busy at work. It never rests. Even when your body and conscious mind are sleeping, your subconscious mind continues to work, day and night, keeping you alive, performing vital tasks far beneath the surface of conscious thinking.

Your subconscious mind is responsible for maintaining involuntary functions in your body. Breathing, cell metabolism, blood circulation and maintenance of vital fluids are a few of the duties carried out constantly, with pinpoint precision, by your subconscious mind. It knows the exact combinations of chemicals and hormones used to create your hair, eyes, ears, nails, teeth, nerve cells—even your brain.

Your subconscious mind can calculate the exact percentage of trace minerals needed in your bloodstream. It maintains your heartbeat at the perfect rate for your level of activity. It instantly computes how these proportions must change if you suddenly start jogging around the block.

The abilities of your subconscious mind cross into the domain of the unknown. It perceives by intuition, sensing many events of which you are consciously un-aware. Your subconscious mind knows far more than your conscious mind. All human secrets are accessible to your subconscious mind.

Your conscious mind and your subconscious mind play very different roles in your life. Listed below are a few qualities associated with these two components of mind.

Conscious mind	Subconscious mind
voluntary behavior	involuntary body functions
intelligence	feelings and emotions
decision making	psychic abilities
logical reasoning	ability to restructure reality
the five senses	link with infinite intelligence

Working together, these two areas of mind serve you well. Each of them has its limitations, and, interestingly, their limitations compliment one another. What the conscious mind can do, the subconscious mind cannot, and what the subconscious mind can do, the conscious mind cannot.

Your conscious mind is a master of logic and reasoning. It has tremendous ability to process information and arrive at logical conclusions. But your conscious mind does not have direct power over your environment. It has no ability to influence the world around you. That is the domain of your subconscious mind.

Your subconscious mind possesses the awesome power to shape reality according to your images. But even with this power, it is thoroughly lacking in reasoning ability. It is unable to analyze or evaluate information. Your subconscious mind, as powerful as it is, is utterly incapable of rational decision making.

Using the mind...

In recent years, psychologists have uncovered much about how the subconscious mind works. They have discovered that when thoughts are reinforced and penetrate to subconscious regions of the mind, impressions are made directly in the brain cells. As the subconscious mind monitors the thinking process, it takes the resultant images and implants them directly in the "fabric" of the cerebrum. This process is similar to what an artist does when he or she transfers an image from the world of imagination to the world of canvas.

Once an image is implanted, your subconscious mind begins the task of materializing that image in the external world. It is well qualified to do this; creating reality is its forte.

But remember, your subconscious mind is not the rational part of your mind, and although it can do many things, logical reasoning is not one of them. Your subconscious mind is incapable of evaluating the images it receives. It accepts whatever you give it without passing judgment. Your subconscious mind is receptive like soil, accepting any seed, good or bad, and growing what is planted. You can plant harmful, negative "seeds" in your subconscious mind just as easily as you can plant positive, beneficial ones. This principle is a key to understanding the progression of events that occur in your life.

> *"As ye sow, so shall ye reap."*
> Galatians 6:7

If you plant a seed for a rose bush, does a geranium sprout and grow from that seed? Of course not. Only a rose bush can grow from a rose seed. Likewise, if you feed your subconscious mind a steady diet of a particular thought, that is the thought that takes root and grows. Listen to what I am telling you here. Today, in your subconscious mind, you are sowing the "seeds" that will become the full-grown "plants" of tomorrow.

> *"It is much less what we do than what we think, which fits us for the future."*
> Philip James Bailey

When you give an image to your subconscious mind, you are, in effect, telling it to create that image in reality. Your subconscious mind does not question whether the image would be good or bad for you. Since your subconscious mind has no ability to reason, it is incapable of evaluating that question. It merely does what it is told. That is its nature.

I know of a man who was fascinated with beavers. One day, he captured a wild beaver, took it home and locked it in his living room. His plan was to train the animal and keep it for a pet. That afternoon, the man drove into town to run some errands. A few hours later, he returned home and walked into his living room. Much to his dismay, the beaver had chopped some of the man's furniture into little pieces and carried the pieces into a corner of the room. There, the animal had constructed a perfect dam, even though no stream of water flowed through the room. The message of this story is clear: you cannot stop a beaver from building dams. That is its nature.

Likewise, your subconscious mind restructures reality according to the images you supply. You cannot stop your subconscious mind from doing this, even if you want to. That is its nature.

Now, here's the clincher: you are already using the power of your subconscious mind. You use this creative ability constantly, day and night, whether you know it or not. Sometimes you use this power to create what you want, other times you use it to create what you dread. The good news is: you have a choice. You can use your mind to create what you want. I hope you grasp the importance of what I just said.

"A man's life is what his thoughts make of it."
Marcus Aurelius

In a manner of speaking, your conscious mind is the doorway to your subconscious mind. Who decides what images reach your subconscious mind? You do. You do so with your conscious mind.

Until now, you've probably been unaware of how these two components of mind work. You've probably exerted little, if any, control over the images fed to your subconscious mind. Now that you understand what is happening, you can change that. You can consciously decide what images you want your subconscious mind to receive.

Once you get an image implanted into your subconscious mind, that image soon manifests in your daily life, regardless of what the image contains. Your subconscious mind does not judge the content of any image. It does not examine the pros and cons to determine whether the outcome will be harmful or beneficial to your goals. Your subconscious mind injects no logic into its efforts. It does not know how. It defers to your conscious mind anything that requires logical reasoning. All it does is take what it receives from you and act on it. Much like a computer, which processes data, your subconscious mind processes images without regard to their content.

> *"Images are like highly explosive vibration bombs, which, when set off, shatter the rocks of difficulties and create the change desired."*
> Paramahansa Yogananda

Remember, your subconscious mind operates on the images you supply. It cannot act contrary to what you give it. So, once you know how, you can supply your subconscious mind with images of your choice, images you wish to make real.

Making everything happen...

In the past few years, amazing discoveries have occurred in the field of quantum physics. These new ideas have tremendous implications.

All objects are made of atoms. All atoms are made of subatomic particles. But these particles do not exist in the normal sense of the word. Many subatomic particles are nothing more than probabilities that appear to exist at certain times. In other words, the building blocks of matter are not, themselves, matter.

By using particle accelerators, physicists have discovered that subatomic particles appear to exist only when someone is thinking about them or trying to observe them. When no one is concentrating on them, they are merely waves of mathematical probability. As soon as they receive some form of attention, they flash into existence. This means that subatomic particles, the essence of all matter, are created by sending thoughts in their direction.

The atom is an arrangement of subatomic particles. The only difference between an atom of one substance and an atom of another substance is the arrangement of these particles, these tiny bundles of energy. Therefore, the only difference between one material object and another—between a ten-dollar bill and a rotten apple, for example—is the way energy is arranged.

Albert Einstein proved that energy and matter are interchangeable. Energy from the human mind converts into material substance with ease. The electrical pulsations of your mind are forms of creative energy, which have the power to reproduce in the physical world whatever images they carry with them. This process goes on continually, every second you are alive.

> *"Reality can destroy the dream, why shouldn't the dream destroy reality?"*
> George Moore

Scientific evidence now points to the existence of some sort of thinking "stuff" from which everything is made. This substance, whatever it is, is everywhere, permeating our universe to the depths of interstellar space. Human beings possess the inherent ability to impress ideas upon this formless substance. This process causes the object being imagined to materialize physically. In other words, when you visualize something in your mind, you are calling upon the same resources that created every material object in the universe.

Every event and circumstance in your life is created from energy. These packets of energy proceed from your thoughts and spread like waves from a broadcast tower. Although objects and situations you see around you appear to happen outside you and beyond your influence, according to the latest scientific evidence, this perception is inaccurate. Scientists now believe you are, in the most fundamental sense, making everything happen! The only reasonable theory, based on the evidence we now have, proclaims that thoughts literally create reality.

Tapping the power...

There exists an intelligence that resides in nature. This intelligence has the know-how to create a human baby, complete in every detail. It knows how to produce a chicken from an egg. It knows how to produce a mighty redwood from a tiny cone. It knows how to manage and care for millions of animal species, each with its own needs and functions.

Have you heard about the cuckoo bird? The cuckoo bird flies over the nest of another bird and mentally photographs the size, shape and color of the eggs in the nest. Later, while the mother is away, the cuckoo returns to that nest and lays an egg along side the other eggs. The egg it lays matches the other eggs in every detail. The cuckoo then flies away.

When the mother bird returns to her nest, she acts as an unknowing foster parent and raises the cuckoo's chicks. Some incredible intelligence instructs the cuckoo on how to duplicate the eggs of other birds. Science has not yet figured out the intelligence that guides the cuckoo bird. This same intelligence directs and manages the flow of all life.

This intelligence is the source of all genius. It is the intelligence that creates and sustains every living entity. This same power is directly available to you. Your direct, hot-line connection to this intelligence is your subconscious mind.

This intelligence knows how to manipulate reality to bring your images to life. Whenever you choose, you can tap this power and channel it to serve you. With this incredible asset on your side, you cannot lose.

The possibilities that lie before you when you consider the creative power of your subconscious mind are imponderable. Your subconscious mind serves as a link between you and all creation. It is your ticket to the infinite.

"We say 'seeing is believing,' but actually, we are much better at believing than at seeing. In fact, we are seeing what we believe all the time and only occasionally seeing what we can't believe."
Robert Anton Wilson

Have you noticed how a new idea seems to come from "out of the blue?" Sometimes the idea doesn't even feel like yours. Thomas Edison said he regularly tapped into his subconscious mind when he wanted answers that no other person knew. The Swiss psychologist, Carl Jung, taught that the subconscious mind contains all knowledge that is gathered in one's lifetime, as well as all wisdom of past ages since the dawn of creation! That is the power you are dealing with here. That is the power you can summon for your own personal use. Outrageous, wouldn't you say? Once you glimpse the enormous creative power of your subconscious mind, you'll stand in awe. When you realize that this power is yours to command, you'll tremble with excitement.

For the masses of humanity, this power lies unnoticed. Nonetheless, it is real. Your subconscious mind has unwavering ability to turn your mental images into their physical (and monetary) equivalents, and it is engaged in this creative activity always—even while you sleep, even at this moment. The process is never-ending. Your reality is constantly being restructured on the basis of images you hold within you.

> *"We are what we pretend to be, so we must be careful about what we pretend to be."*
> Kurt Vonnegut, Jr.

Mark Twain said, "Life does not consist mainly, or even largely, of facts and happenings. It consists mainly of the stream of thought that is forever flowing through one's head." Your subconscious mind has infinite power at its disposal to create a world based on your mental images. In fact, it has all the power that exists. *Your* mind! Yes, you! Little ol' you, and your little ol' mind! Sounds incredible, but it's a fact.

Your subconscious mind is exceedingly wise. It knows things that have never been written in books. It has access to information not yet discovered. In some unknown and mysterious way, your subconscious mind is intimately linked to the source of all intelligence. You owe it to yourself to use this power, to tap into this mighty resource, to put this tremendous asset to work for you in order to get what you want from life.

Shaping reality...

Have you ever wondered why your life is the way it is? Why must you struggle to exist? Why do so many circumstances seem stacked against you? Why do you not have enough money to do everything you want? Why is lack of money an obstacle to your happiness? Why is this world so difficult? Why are things so weird?

The answer to all these questions is simple. The reason your world is the way it is, is because that's the way you *think* your world is. Got that? At the subconscious level, you hold certain images you are unaware of. Your world is a perfect reflection of those images. The only reason why the circumstances of your life are as they are is because that is how you think they are.

"Those people who think they can do something and those who think they can't are both right."
Henry Ford

You are the sum of all your thoughts. Your thoughts, whatever they are, when held long enough, materialize into reality. An idea fixed in your mind shapes the future. Your health, your success and your financial situation are not simply matters of work, play and active pursuits. What you do is secondary; the circumstances of your life proceed from the source. The primary source is always a matter of mind. The subconscious mind deals in realms far beyond ordinary comings and goings.

Responsibility for your subconscious mind rests with you alone. You must decide whether you want to use this power to your benefit or to your detriment. Destructive, frustrating ideas held in your subconscious mind insure that you have destructive, frustrating experiences in life. Successful, prosperous ideas insure successful, prosperous experiences in life. This cause-and-effect relationship cannot be subverted. Adherence to your images is the way your life has always functioned, and always will.

"Hold a picture of yourself long enough in your mind's eye and you will be drawn toward it."
Dr. Harry Emerson Fosdick

When you feed your subconscious mind an image of yourself as unsociable and unattractive, you lead a lonely life. When you tell your subconscious that you are stupid and inept, you create a lifetime of failure and insignificance. When you give your subconscious a vision of greed and jealousy, you experience difficulty holding on to possessions. When you implant a subconscious image of yourself as sick and diseased, you manifest one illness after another. When you hold a mental picture of poverty and deprivation, you suffer continual problems with money, no matter what you do.

When you feed your subconscious mind an image of yourself as likeable and attractive, you have plenty of friends. When you tell your subconscious that you are intelligent and quick-witted, your accomplishments showcase your mental abilities. When you give your subconscious a vision of love and understanding, you attract whatever relationships you desire. When you implant a subconscious image of yourself as healthy and resistant to disease, you lead a long and vigorous life. When you hold a mental picture of wealth and abundance, you live prosperously, and money does not concern you.

"To be a hero think heroic thoughts."
Voltaire

If you consistently impress upon your subconscious mind that you are unlucky and unsuccessful, a huge amount of creative energy is working against your best interest, making success unlikely for you. No matter what you do, your subconscious mind sees to it that, somehow, you fail. Reality will always conform to your subconscious images.

When you change your images, your life changes along with them. When you impress upon your subconscious mind the image that luck is running your way and that you are successful, good fortune is certain. Then, no matter what you do, you will unleash positive energy toward the manifestation of a prosperous life.

> "*The greatest discovery of my generation is that human beings, by changing the inner attitudes of their minds, can change the outer aspects of their lives.*"
> William James

Unhappy images make you unhappy. Sick images make you sick. Poor and fearful images lead to failure and keep you in poverty. By learning direct control over the images you implant into your subconscious mind, you can assure that only positive images take effect. By doing so, you can restructure your life, your body, your financial situation and your whole environment.

This is not an opinion. What I am telling you is fact. Your subconscious mind holds strong images about your success or failure. These are images you have supplied for years. Now, from this moment forth, the nature of your subconscious images is up to you. You have control over what new images you want to plant. You decide.

Storing images...

If everyone in the world had already supplied his or her subconscious mind with a feast of constructive images, the information in this book would be unnecessary. If everyone were already happy and wealthy, then I'd be wasting my time writing this material. No one would want to learn how to create positive mental images if everyone already had everything life could offer.

Obviously, such is not the case. Greed, sickness, misery, starvation and unhappiness abound. Individual and worldwide poverty increase every year. Negativity is the predominant attitude on earth. Clearly, many destructive images are being held in subconscious minds. The images are already there. This state of affairs may be hard to admit, but the facts speak for themselves.

Where did all these negative images come from? How did you manage to get destructive images implanted into your subconscious mind? Let me tell you something about conditioning.

A man went to work one day, and several of his friends at the office decided to mess with his mind. One by one, they made comments to him implying he looked sick. They said things like, "Hey, Joe, are you feeling alright?" Throughout the day, they kept a constant barrage of negative suggestions about his health coming his way.

At the end of the day, someone asked him how he felt. His reply? "Not so well."

Joe had become "conditioned" to a particular way of thinking. By continually harping on one specific idea, his associates had caused Joe to feel a certain way. When a thought is repeated often enough, anyone can fall prey to this type of conditioning.

> *"Most people are about as happy as they make up their mind to be."*
> Abraham Lincoln

Conditioning is most effective when directed at children. Their minds are receptive and impressionable. They believe what they are told, whether or not the message is true. And with children, impressions last. Children who are conditioned—through words or actions—that they are stupid and ineffectual grow up to be just that. Studies prove it.

Think back to when you were a child. Did your parents ever complain about money? Did they say people must work hard to earn a living? Did they indicate they thought money was hard to come by? Did their actions convey the feeling that money is a serious matter? All these messages are picked up by the child and serve to condition the young person at a subconscious level. The child does not notice what is happening at the time, but these messages get through and leave their cruel mark on the child's mind and personality.

As youngsters, most of us conclude subconsciously that money is a problem. We hear from parents, teachers and relatives that money is difficult to make and accumulate. An idea given to a child—even if presented nonverbally—sinks quickly and easily to the subconscious level. The idea then manifests throughout life. That is why so many people in our society have serious issues surrounding money.

Once you become conditioned, your experience in the real world validates your belief that acquiring money is difficult. Jobs become hard to find and keep. Bill paying becomes a struggle. You barely make ends meet. You find money impossible to save. Money worries eventually consume you, and you fall deep into debt. You end up feeling gypped, as if conned by society.

> *"Our doubts are traitors and make us lose
> the good we oft might win."*
> William Shakespeare

Do you have all the money you need or want right now? Are you independently wealthy? Have you created an abundant flow of money into your life? Is money of no concern to you? Have you solved all your money problems forever? I'll bet not. Chances are, you do not now have all the money you'd like to have. I make this guess based on the fact that you purchased this book. I am willing to bet that you are not now financially secure. Am I right? If so, then I have proven that, at this moment, you are storing negative images in your mind, images that poison your thoughts about yourself and money.

Psychological tests show that most people tend to minimize themselves. You probably have some sub-conscious feelings of inadequacy or inferiority. These feelings are usually thrust upon us at an early age by our parents and other adults. Although the intensity varies from one individual to another, no person alive today is totally free of any such feelings.

This fact is not intended to downgrade your parents or teachers. They behaved unknowingly. They were un-aware that they were sending negative impressions to vulnerable young minds. This type of conditioning occurs just by nature of being raised in our contemporary so-ciety. Our guardians and authorities mean well, but they unwittingly create an atmosphere of negativity and hope-lessness. This is unfortunate, but undeniably true in our modern-day world.

Shooting for the stars...

Somehow, negative images have gotten into your subconscious mind. Have no doubt, they are there. Right now, they are in you, me, and everyone around us. You do not need to do anything special to get them. All you need to do is be born, survive the rigors of childhood and go forth into the world. Rest assured, you've already been supplied with your fair share of hurtful and destructive images in your precious subconscious mind.

These images regulate your life, casting you into a lifetime of poverty, discontent and self-debasement. Yes, old thoughts continue to influence your life, even if you no longer think them consciously. Your subconscious mind remembers.

Sounds pretty grim, right? Not at all. I have some good news for you: *you can change!* No matter how terrible the situation looks at this moment, things are not hopeless. Hope exists because you can change the images planted in your subconscious mind.

CHANGE IS POSSIBLE!

When an image becomes implanted in your subconscious mind, it stays there *only until it is eliminated or replaced*. Your childhood images of fear, poverty, and unhappiness cease to control your life as soon as you replace them with other images you prefer. You know what that means? It means you have another chance. It means you have major cause for celebration. Be consoled by the fact that you can change your life. You can start over and shoot for the stars.

Make no mistake about it, negative images are already rooted in your subconscious mind. To repair your life, you must supplant them with positive ones. You must take charge of the images stored within you. You must intentionally implant the images you want. This you can do. I'll show you how.

4

Implanting
Your Images

IF I WERE TO TURN you loose right now and tell you to go forth and plant all kinds of wonderful images in your subconscious mind, how would you do it? Would you drop a photograph into a slot somewhere? Would you visit a pharmacist and request a magic pill? Would you ask your attorney to draw up appropriate papers? As you might guess, none of these approaches would have any effect whatsoever. Your subconscious mind is a subtle mechanism, and you need to know the right way to reach it.

Cultivating positive images...

An effective method of implanting images must be based on an accurate understanding of how your subconscious mind works. You need to know what makes it accessible and what makes it respond. You need to know what makes it tick. When you treat your subconscious mind the right way, it behaves in a manner that is reliable and predictable.

The images you wish to implant into your subconscious mind must be presented in a way that they can be received and processed. For your efforts to succeed, the images must be communicated using the "language" of your subconscious mind.

You'll be happy to know that the right way to do this has already been discovered; all the research has been done for you. The procedure I am about to describe works perfectly. The method is easy to perform, and it gets the job done. If you follow the instructions I give, precisely as I outline them, you will implant images of your choice firmly into the fabric of your subconscious mind.

If you feel you can reach your subconscious mind and plant positive images without the aid of this method, fine. I say more power to you. I would wager, however, that you cannot do this. That is why you need these instructions to accomplish the task of implanting your images.

*"Doctor, I wrestled with reality for forty years,
and I am happy to state that I finally won."*
James Stewart, in *Harvey*

What you are trying to do here is tricky. Implanting your images is not hard, but it requires finesse. I know how to do it, and I am happy to share my knowledge with you. I will give you complete, step-by-step, easy-to-understand instructions for a simple, yet surefire, technique. This technique is designed for the express purpose of getting your images implanted.

The principles involved have stood the test of time. In one form or another, these principles have been used since the dawn of humankind. Many successful people have made use of positive images to achieve their goals.

Here is a sampling of individuals who have espoused the effectiveness of cultivating positive images.

Benjamin Franklin	F. W. Woolworth
John D. Rockefeller	Michael Jordan
Alexander Graham Bell	Theodore Roosevelt
Rose Kennedy	George Harrison
Andrew Carnegie	Shirley MacLaine
Henry David Thoreau	Ken Griffey, Jr.
Muhammad Ali	Julius Rosenwald
Bill Gates	Woodrow Wilson
John Denver	Earl Nightengale
Thomas Edison	Henry Ford
Mary Lou Retton	William Howard Taft
Luther Burbank	Stevie Wonder
William Jennings Bryan	Arthur Nash
Conrad Hilton	Sharon Stone
Albert Einstein	George Eastman
Oprah Winfrey	Mahatma Gandhi
Abraham Lincoln	William Wrigley, Jr.

Truth is, I could fill an entire book with names such as these. Literally thousands upon thousands of successful individuals have put into practice a technique like the one I am about to reveal.

The method I describe in this book has been tested and retested by a large number of people over a period of many years. After much research and refinement, the method is perfected. I give it to you now in its final form.

Every time you use this technique, you will witness irrefutable results. It is a foolproof way of informing your subconscious mind that, from now on, you expect big money to flow into your life. Practice this technique exactly as I say, and you will definitely implant images of wealth and success into your mind. This will increase your attractive force toward money and lead to a life of financial ease.

Expecting the ultimate...

Have you ever felt that certain people have good luck, and that other people have nothing but tough breaks? Have you ever wondered why the world seems so unfair to some people? Here's the deal. What most people think of as good luck or bad luck is, in fact, the direct, manifested result of images implanted in their subconscious mind. Luck, fate and chance are illusory concepts. People with positive images have good luck; people with negative images have bad luck. That's all. Instead of attributing what happens to Lady Luck, you will do much better to create your own good fortune.

> *"There is no such thing as luck, only preparation meeting opportunity."*
> Vince Lombardi

A number of years ago, I was invited to visit a sales training program for a marketing company. They conducted an experiment. One training class was told to expect a certain level of sales per month. Another class was told to expect a level of sales exactly double what the first class was told. All other aspects of the training were identical for both classes.

After their first month in the field, the second group had outsold the first group by a ratio of nearly two to one. I ask you, were they luckier? Was the second group getting all the breaks while the first group was having a run of bad luck? Hardly.

After examining the company's employee records, I discovered that each salesperson earned about the same amount each month as they did the preceding month. There were fluctuations and tendencies, but, overall, a salesperson's monthly figure did not vary much from his or her average. I also uncovered that certain individuals made nearly all their sales during the first half of the month. The second half of the month, they showed up for work and went through the motions, but did not produce significant sales. Meanwhile, other salespeople made most of their sales in the second half of the month and almost none in the first half. The pattern remained consistent for each salesperson, month after month.

How can these observations be explained? A theory based on chance does not explain figures so consistent over an extended period of time. Here's the explanation: Each salesperson earned exactly what he or she *expected* to earn. What the person *wanted* to make had no bearing on sales. What the person *hoped* to make proved irrelevant. The only criterion that mattered was what the person honestly *expected* to make.

YOU GET OUT OF LIFE EXACTLY WHAT YOU EXPECT AT THE SUBCONSCIOUS LEVEL.

What happens in your life is not necessarily what you would *wish* to happen. What happens is what you subconsciously *expect* to happen. So, if the images in your subconscious mind show a prosperous and fun-filled life, you experience what people call good luck. Things go your way. If, on the other hand, the images in your subconscious mind show an unsuccessful and unsatisfying life, you experience bad luck. No matter what you try to accomplish, unfortunate circumstances beyond your control pop up and frustrate you. People feel sorry for you because you are so darned unlucky.

Don't get caught in this cycle of self-pity. You can create success instead. You can implant images you want, break the cycle and make your life unfold as you choose. Once you know how, you can consciously supply the images your mind uses to form its expectations. You can take charge of your future. You can leave the losers on their way down—and join the winners on their way up.

Millions of people believe they are doomed to a life of hard times and failure. They are convinced that their sad state of affairs is mandated by some strange force that lies beyond their control. Little do they realize, they are the creators of their own misfortune. Their unhappy life is the direct result of the images they carry within. All that's happening is that their subconscious minds are translating their images into reality.

*"Man is not the creature of circumstances.
Circumstances are the creature of man."*
Benjamin Disraeli

Many years ago, I knew an old man who seemed to be very unlucky. He seemed to have more than his share of bad breaks. His life was one long series hard-luck stories. I remember, he was always saying, "Well, that's life." Whenever something went wrong, he'd shrug his shoulders and mutter, "Well, that's life."

No! The man was wrong. That is not life. That is not how life has to be—not unless you choose to think so. Life does not need to be one long series of bad breaks and broken dreams. Life does not need to be an endless and thankless struggle, all the way to the poorhouse.

Life can be a beautiful and exciting journey, leading to the land of serenity and happiness.

You have a fundamental right to success and good fortune. Expect it! Really, expect it. Forget the scorn and ridicule of the wisecrackers and hopeless Johnny's. You'll soon leave them in the dust anyway. Imagine the most outrageous, pleasure-filled life possible—and then expect it. Expect the ultimate! Expect it and you will have it.

> *"If ye have faith, ye shall say unto this mountain,*
> *move hence to yonder place; and it shall move;*
> *and nothing shall be impossible unto you."*
> Matthew 17:20

Your expectations need to exist at the subconscious level. You cannot fake this. Only what you sincerely expect, deep in your mind, counts. In the following pages, I will show you how to plant images at this deep level of mind. When you do so, you'll be giving your subconscious mind the images it will use when forming expectations.

By practicing this method, you will rid your mind of hard-luck thoughts. *Just my luck! That figures! Why me, Lord?* Your new images will replace thoughts like these with confident, reassuring thoughts. *Everything is going my way. I can do anything. Look out, man!*

Feel the excitement. Let yourself itch with anticipation for changes soon to come. It won't be long. Once your subconscious mind expects something, you're just a short time away from having it.

Taking control...

You pick: either you voluntarily plant into your subconscious mind the images you select, the images you want to manifest, or your mind feeds on whatever images reach it as a result of your neglect. There exists no shortage of bleak, poverty-ridden images waiting to take root. Your subconscious mind will not lie idle. It will surely find something to do.

If you get nothing else from this chapter, get this:

YOU CAN VOLUNTARILY IMPLANT INTO YOUR SUBCONSCIOUS MIND ANY IMAGE YOU SO DESIRE.

The sooner you realize the potential implied in the above statement, the sooner you will find relief from your frustration. At this moment, you possess the capability to grab hold of your life and point it in the direction you want. When you implant images of your choosing, you are taking concrete steps to shape your destiny and create the world of your dreams.

Maybe you have a defeatist attitude. Maybe you even acknowledge your defeatist attitude. Most people give up when they become aware they have an unhealthy outlook. They realize their attitude is self-defeating and, since they have no idea how to fix it, they become depressed and discouraged. They resign themselves to a lifetime of struggle and unhappiness. In time, they lose hope. They become bitter.

Don't you. Don't you dare! Just because you do not now have the positive outlook you want does not mean that such an attitude is unattainable for you. You can change all that, and quickly. Your mind is not something that gets locked into place and becomes impossible to alter. Your mental pictures are easily rebuilt, repaired and entirely overhauled.

You are not the problem here. You are fine the way you are. The images that have slipped into your subconscious mind are the problem. They are what determine your fate.

You do not have to be broke. You do not have to be struggling and unhappy. You are not the dregs of the earth. You are a beautiful creation, the pride and joy of the universe. You carry within you unlimited potential. You deserve to be rich. You deserve to be happy. You were not meant to fret away your time on this planet, wasting your life over petty concerns about money. You have better things to do.

Breathe a sigh of relief. You can fix your life. By implanting into your subconscious mind images you select, instructions go forth into the real world to materialize exactly what you want. Reality restructures itself to accommodate your images. Amazingly, what you heretofore thought of as unchangeable, changes before your eyes.

Any image you implant into your subconscious mind surely becomes reality, every bit as solid as the concrete that forms the foundation of your home. Regardless of what image you implant, that idea is, somehow, in some way, made manifest. This occurs in reality! That is how creation works.

"You must give birth to your images. They are the future waiting to be born."
Rainer Maria Rilke

Everything that exists in your material world is the work of intelligent creation. Your physical body and everything you experience in life are the result of ideas transformed into visible reality.

This is not an outlandish concept. The fact that thoughts shape reality is a universal truth. The idea may sound weird or esoteric to you, but it cannot be denied. Your life is your choice. You can either implant the images you want materialized, or you can do nothing and let your subconscious mind materialize what it has already been given in the past. Take your pick.

To change your life, all you need to do is find out exactly what you want, implant that image into your subconscious mind and hold it there long enough for it to become reality. This approach puts the power of the universe on your side. Get that power working *for* you, toward the realization of your goals, instead of working *against* you, toward your undoing.

"Unless you change direction, you are likely
to end up where you are headed."
Chinese proverb

Are you happy with your life? In other words, are you satisfied with the images you hold in your subconscious mind? If not, then change them. If you do not change the course you are on, you have no one to blame but yourself. Take comfort in the fact that you can change everything whenever you are ready.

THE HUMAN BEING IS SO CONSTRUCTED
THAT IT HAS ABSOLUTE CONTROL
OVER THE COMMANDS THAT REACH
ITS SUBCONSCIOUS MIND.

There is great responsibility implied in the above statement. Sure, you may have had some bad breaks in the past. Sure, you may have been born into poverty.

Sure, you may have failed before. But, as of this moment, you have the information you need to change all that. Your life, from here on out, is your responsibility. If you deny the situation or make up excuses, your inaction condemns you to a life of continued struggle. If you own up to your potential and do something about your situation, you reap phenomenal benefit. This matter is your responsibility—and your choice.

> *"Failure and success are not accidents but the strictest of justice."*
> Alexander Smith

I assume you prefer to live without money-related stress, without financial worry. I suspect that is why you purchased this book in the first place. If so, your path is clear. You must embark on a course of implanting images. Your task is to implant specific images of wealth and prosperity into the fertile soil of your subconscious mind.

Implanting your images is all that is required of you; your subconscious mind will do the rest. Don't worry, nothing can hinder the tremendous power of your subconscious mind. No task is too great. Whatever needs doing, consider it done. Your success is assured.

> The mighty oak tree sleeps within the acorn. Your future success is sleeping now within your subconscious mind.

Congratulations. From now on, you will be taking control of the images that reach your subconscious mind. From this day forth, your life will be different than it has ever been, financially and every other way. Your success is as certain as the fact that I am writing this.

Implanting images of your choice into your subconscious mind is the most powerful and effective course of action you could ever pursue. How do you do this? What procedure do you use for implanting your images? How do you "get to" your subconscious mind? These are good questions. You are, no doubt, curious by now. I've been promising to tell you the details, and I will keep my promise.

5

Affirmations

MARK THIS DAY ON YOUR calendar. This is the day you first heard of the magic process called "affirmations." Many people swear that the discovery of affirmations is, without question, the single most significant event in their lifetime. Someday you, too, will realize the magnitude of what you are about to learn.

Please, do not let the term *affirmations* scare you. Do not be put off or intimidated. The procedure is easy to do and requires no special skill.

Can you read and write? If you are reading this book, the answer is yes. Can you count to three? If you passed first grade, I bet you can. All right then, you have all the skills required to use the power of affirmations.

Assembling a wish list...

Now, I would like you to do a simple writing exercise. Get a pencil and paper, and prepare to write. Do it now. Are you ready?

I am going to ask you one simple question. On a blank piece of paper or in the space below, write the first thing that comes to your mind in response to the this question. The question is:

What do you want?

_____

_____

If my guess is correct, the space above is still blank and you are reading this now even though you did not write anything down. Am I right?

What thoughts occurred to you when you read the question? The question is easy to understand; it contains four simple words. Most people, as soon as they read the question, experience a flood of ideas, a rush of thoughts without order. In the confusion, they find it difficult to formulate a coherent answer. As a result, they give up and read on without answering.

This lack of clarity is precisely the problem. You do not know exactly what you want. You do not have a clear and specific image of your desires. This uncertainty is, by far, the number-one reason that most people are not happy or successful. Surveys show that only two out of every one thousand people have a clear idea of what they want in their lives.

MOST OF US GO THROUGH LIFE NOT KNOWING WHAT WE WANT...BUT FEELING DARNED SURE WE DON'T HAVE IT!

A general feeling of dissatisfaction should not, in any way, be mistaken for knowing what you want. Most people are dissatisfied with their life. There's nothing unique in that. Precious few, however, have the slightest idea what they want.

Suppose a man decides to take a plane trip on his vacation. He goes to the airport and the following conversation takes place between him and the ticket agent.

"Hello, I'd like to buy a ticket."

"Okay, fine. Where would you like to go?"

"Well, I'm not really sure."

"You want to buy a ticket, and you don't even know where to?"

"Yeah, I guess that's right."

"Well, I'm sorry, but I can't help you unless you know where you want to go."

"Oh, I don't really care, just someplace where I can have a good time."

"Sorry, sir. You need to know where you want to go. If you tell me that, I can get you there. Otherwise, I can't help you. I'd like to, but I can't."

This ridiculous conversation is the type of dialog most people have with their subconscious mind. Their mind would like to help them, but it can't. If they knew what they wanted, their subconscious mind could get it for them, but they haven't a clue about what they want. A philosopher once said that muddled thoughts mean a muddled life. You don't want to go on like that, do you? If not, your state of befuddlement must end now.

> The first step toward *getting* what
> you want is *knowing* what you want.

Maybe you wish you were somewhere other than where you are right now. Maybe you wish you were doing something different than what you do these days. Maybe you wish you owned more things than you own at this time. These feelings are general and ambiguous, not clear and precise. These thoughts are not the same as specific images. To get results, you must know exactly where you want to be, what you want to be doing and what things you want to own. Only when you know details, can you form images of what you want.

Suppose a genie appeared before you and said, "I will grant your wishes. Make a list for me." What would you wish for? How would you go about assembling a wish list? Do you know?

A man once told me, "I yearn for something. I long for it with all my heart. I just don't know what it is." Do you ever feel that way? If so, you are not alone. You join millions of others who have no idea what they want. I say: You have felt that way long enough. It's time to do something about your situation. It's time to find out exactly what you want.

Going hog-wild...

I am going to ask you the same question again. Only this time, you will answer it.

What do you want?

As we proceed now, do not trouble yourself with whether you think you can obtain any of these things. All you need to concern yourself with is determining what you want. After you know *what* you want, I'll show you how to get it. Realize that your subconscious mind does not respond to ambiguity. You must be specific.

Get your pen or pencil ready. If you prefer not to write in this book or you need more room, use your own paper for the following exercises.

You will make two lists. The first list contains your most pressing needs. The second list deals with your ultimate desires. Let's begin. And, this time, do it!

On the next page are more blank spaces. In the left-hand column, write what comes to mind when you think of your immediate money problems. You should consider your monetary situation as it stands right now, today. State each problem briefly, but be specific. For example, don't write, "bills." Write which specific bills you find pressing at this moment. Fill in the left-hand column first. You do not need to fill in all the spaces; if only a few things come to mind, that's okay.

When you feel you've listed your major problems, then proceed down the right-hand column and write what you think would be a satisfying solution to each problem. This may require some thought. You may need to make a few decisions, such as whether a broken object should be repaired or replaced. In creating this list, you are concerned with seeking only adequate solutions to your immediate money problems. The solutions on this list should bring your financial situation to the level of "getting by" or "treading water."

I'll give you a few examples. Do *not* copy these examples and use them as your own.

PROBLEMS	ACCEPTABLE SOLUTIONS
car needs tune up	car tuned up and running
dentist bill of $480	bill paid in full
couch falling apart	new couch
loan payment overdue	paid, late charges too
dryer broken	dryer repaired
Billy's shoes worn out	$150 tennis shoes for Billy
need new eyeglasses	new teardrop-style glasses

Now, you do it. List your most pressing financial problems, then write what you consider an acceptable solution to each. Know that by writing these items in black-and-white, you are taking the first step toward tangible solutions in real life. Now, make your list. Go to it!

PROBLEMS   ACCEPTABLE SOLUTIONS

Your first list is now complete. You have stated your immediate financial needs and compiled a list of acceptable solutions. The items on this list are the first installment of what you want.

Now, you are going to have some real fun. You can go hog-wild on this next list.

This time, list whatever comes to mind when you think of things you want. This is not a list of what you need, but a list of what you desire. These can be things you are nowhere near achieving at the present time. Look ahead and picture your life exactly as you wish it to be. Do not be timid. Do not limit yourself. List extravagances. If you want something, list it.

Be as specific as you possibly can. Do not write, "lots of money." Write, "500,000 dollars a year." Do not write, "a nice job." Write, "a position as a lab technician." Do not write, "a fun vacation." Write, "a trip to Europe for one month." Do not write, "a good car." Write, "a new red BMW 840." Do not write, "prestige." Write "president of the local Citizens Caucus." Write your ideas in the order they come to you. Here are some examples:

WANTS

$850,000 home, in woods, fireplace
new red BMW 840
$3,500 Pioneer CD stereo system
Dodge mini-van, fully furnished
$500,000 bank balance
trip to Europe for one month
Ross diamond necklace from Hogan's
$500,000 per year income
to be close friends with Joe and Sue
24-foot sailboat, equipped
masters degree in psychology from UCLA

Now, it's your turn. List your wants. Include whatever comes to mind, regardless of whether obtaining the item seems reasonable. And have fun doing this.

WANTS

_____

_____

_____

_____

_____

_____

_____

_____

_____

_____

_____

_____

_____

_____

_____

_____

_____

You have now created two lists. Taken together, your ACCEPTABLE SOLUTIONS and your WANTS make up a description of items you desire. The next step is to give these items further consideration.

Answering the question...

You will now examine every item on both lists. The purpose here is to reduce the total number of items by eliminating those that don't meet the following criteria. Evaluate each of your items in accordance with these five considerations:

(1) Do you *really* want it?

Do not list a particular item because you think most people would want it. Do not list it because you remember wanting it in the past. Do not list it because the words look impressive on paper. Do you honestly want it? Your likelihood of getting the item should not play into this evaluation; your only consideration here is whether or not you sincerely want it.

You must have a burning desire for the item, not a casual interest in it. You must want the thing so badly you can almost taste it. When you think of the item, you should feel an emotional response. If not, eliminate it. Your final list should contain only items you want badly. Do not be reluctant to drop many or most of your items as a result of this consideration. Be tough. Eliminate all weak items. When you come across an item you truly want, you'll recognize it.

(2) Is it realistically possible?

The only consideration here is that the item be humanly possible to obtain. Do not concern yourself with whether you deem it feasible right now. No item is unrealistic if anyone has ever achieved it at any time in the past. For example, it is unrealistic to swim to Hawaii, but it is well within the realm of possibility to take a trip to Hawaii on your new yacht.

(3) Will anyone be harmed by it?

Do not worry about whether your neighbors would be jealous. That is not the type of "harm" meant here. This consideration refers to actual, malicious—physical or mental—damage to another individual. For example, someone would be harmed if you were to own a shrunken head of your mother-in-law.

(4) Does it contradict any other item on your list?

Does the fulfillment of the item in question preclude the fulfillment of any other item? Do any two items on your list pull your energy in opposite directions? For example, if you want to be a professional jockey and, at the same time, want to win the heavyweight boxing championship, you need to eliminate one of these items from your list. The occurrence of conflicting items is uncommon, but important to check for.

(5) Is it enough?

This consideration is tricky. The essential idea is: *do not limit yourself*. Most people go through life with a cautious and limiting attitude toward everything. That is unfortunate because their constant wariness holds them back. Courage, not caution, is the quality that is called for here.

Be alert to your negative conditioning. Suppose you want an income of $500,000 a year. However, a few moments ago, when you wrote down the amount, you got hit with a flash of timidity. Instead of writing $500,000, you wrote $200,000. Change it! Write what you really want, as long as the item is realistic (as defined in the second of these five considerations). Do not limit yourself. Although you may find this concept difficult, you must abandon the limitations you have lived with thus far in your life. You must force yourself to think big.

REACH LOW—BORING.
REACH HIGH—SOARING!

Let's try an experiment. In the space below, write your yearly income at the present time:

$ _____ .00

Now, in the following space, write the amount you *want* your yearly income to be:

$ _____ .00

Compare the two figures. Is your desired income a measly few thousand dollars more than the amount you presently earn? Would you honestly be satisfied with that minuscule improvement? As a general rule, your desired income should be, at the very least, double your current income. If the second figure above is not twice as big as the first, then you are aiming too low. Cross out the number right now and write in a figure you can be proud of.

Set your goals high. This is no place for wimpiness. If an item seems unattainable, so much the better. List anything you want, regardless of what it is. Be bold.

Now, in the space below, write all the items from your previous two lists that pass the scrutiny of these five considerations.

WHAT DO YOU WANT?

_____

_____

_____

_____

_____

_____

_____

_____

_____

_____

_____

_____

_____

_____

_____

_____

Now you've done something! You've answered the question: *What do you want?* Your answer is specific, and you've put it in writing. You are now ready to convert each of your wants into the form of an affirmation.

Selecting the words...

An affirmation is a sentence that makes a specific statement about yourself as though the statement were already true. An affirmation is created for the purpose of implanting the expressed image into your subconscious mind. Here is an example of an affirmation: "I, John, own a new red BMW 840."

To be effective, an affirmation must be:

(1) Specific
(2) Positive

Both of these qualities are essential. First, an affirmation must be specific. The content of the affirmation must be expressed in sufficient detail for you to easily visualize it. When creating an affirmation, think of every possible aspect of the particular item. Include whatever details are significant to you and write them down.

Let's say you want a new house. Don't write, "a new house." Some aspects to consider are the location (what city, what part of the city), the type of home (two-story, ranch), the number of rooms (bedrooms, bathrooms), the general design, the furnishings, the color, the fireplace, the yard and so forth. Take a hard look at any features that help you visualize the house in detail. You need to get a clear picture of the place, a feel for it.

To write a good affirmation, analyze and investigate. Decide on specifics. Do not write, "plenty of money." Be definite about the amount. Write, "$500,000." If you want a new stereo system but don't know what kind, find out. Learn what you need to know. Visit a stereo store and study some literature. Talk to sales people and listen to demo systems. Do not write, "a stereo system." Write, "a $3,500 Pioneer CD stereo system." Make sure every affirmation you create is specific enough for you to see the item in your mind.

In addition to being specific, an affirmation must be positive. Writing a positive affirmation is not as simple as it sounds or as obvious as you may think. Sometimes, an affirmation appears to be positive when it is not.

Your subconscious mind takes everything literally. It believes what you say—exactly what the words mean. This may or may not be what you intend to say. For this reason, proper wording is critical.

An affirmation must be stated *as though the fact were already accomplished.* This requirement is vitally important. The wording may seem awkward to you at first, but you'll get the hang of it.

Let's assume you want a new $3,500 Pioneer CD stereo system. Your affirmation should read, "I, John, own a new $3,500 Pioneer CD stereo system."

Never write, "I, John, want a new $3,500 Pioneer CD stereo system." Your subconscious mind hears this statement and realizes that if you *want* it, you do not now *have* it. Thus, the image that gets implanted into your subconscious mind is: "I, John, do not now own a $3,500 Pioneer CD stereo system." Notice that the result of this affirmation turns out to be negative. By the time the idea gets to your subconscious mind, it carries the exact opposite meaning from what you intended. Much of your thinking probably focuses on what you do not have. Your affirmations must not reinforce this thinking.

By the same reasoning, do not write, "I, John, wish I had a new $3,500 Pioneer CD stereo system," or "I, John, need a new $3,500 Pioneer CD stereo system." These affirmations are negative. The message your mind gets is that you do not now have the stereo system you want.

Do not even write, "I, John, will own a new $3,500 Pioneer CD stereo system." This affirmation can fool you because it sounds positive. However, your subconscious mind figures that, since you *will* own one, you must *not now* own one. As a result, the image of you owning the stereo system never goes anywhere. The image that actually gets implanted is one of you not now owning a new $3,500 Pioneer CD stereo system.

A large number of people have tested various forms of affirmations over a period of decades. The evidence is conclusive that any affirmation written from a negative vantage point is ineffective. The only form of affirmation that works is the form in which the item is described *as though you already have it at this moment*. Express your affirmation like this: "I, John, own a new $3,500 Pioneer CD stereo system." Your subconscious mind hears this statement, and the image of you owning the stereo system gets implanted. If you put your affirmations in this form, they will work.

Do not use negative language in the wording of any affirmation. Avoid words such as "no," "not," "never" and so forth. An affirmation should describe something you want to attract, not something you want to avoid. Do not write, "I, John, do not have a pain in my shoulder." Instead write, "I, John, have cured the pain in my shoulder," or "I, John, have a healthy shoulder that is free from pain." Always express your affirmations from a positive point of view.

In a sense, you are trying to "trick" your subconscious mind into believing that the thought expressed is true. That is easy to do if you word your affirmation properly. Your subconscious mind responds to clarity and assertiveness, not wishful thinking. That is why these two requirements—specific and positive—are essential.

Always insert your name in your affirmations. If you have more than one name or, for any reason, you feel uncertain about what name you should use, use whatever name is current in your life, the name you respond to these days.

I recommend that you do not use the word "we" as the subject of an affirmation. For example, do not write, "We, John and Lisa, have a healthy baby girl." Your subconscious mind focuses energy on your individual reality far more effectively than on collective realities. Write, "I, John, have a healthy baby girl with my wife Lisa." Some people claim success using "we" in their affirmations, but many others find such affirmations ineffective. I advise you to play it safe and use only yourself as the subject of your affirmations.

Each affirmation can be as long or as short as you want, provided you feel comfortable with the length. Keep in mind, however, you will be writing these affirmations repeatedly. For that reason, you may prefer to keep them short. As a general rule, make your affirmations as brief as possible without sacrificing clarity. For example, instead of writing, "I, John, am now dating Mary Schlessinger," you can get away with, "I, John, am now dating Mary," provided you know who you mean and you visualize only the intended person when you write the affirmation. Length is a matter of personal preference, and you will probably prefer short.

The following are a few examples of properly worded affirmations:

I, John, have a new Kenmore dryer in the basement.

I, John, live in a $850,000 redwood home, located in the woods outside town.

I, John, wear a set of teardrop-style, gold-metal eyeglasses.

I, John, own a new red BMW 840.

I, John, have a soft-blue, early-American couch in the south corner of my living room.

I, John, have a $500,000 bank balance.

I, John, own a new $3,500 Pioneer CD stereo system with separate speakers upstairs.

I, John, earn $500,000 a year.

I, John, have paid Dr. Kessler's $480 dentist bill.

I, John, feel healthy and energetic all the time.

Do not copy these examples and use them as your own. Your affirmations will be different. Create your affirmations based on your unique desires. Let your individuality show when selecting the words.

Some books and seminars supply generic affirmations and recommend that you use them. You can use them if you like, but such affirmations are never as effective as ones you create yourself. Samples can be helpful in the process of formulating affirmations, but that's all. With this caveat in mind, I have included a few sample affirmations in the back of this book.

Appendix A (pg. 243) contains a short list of general affirmations. However, I caution you: do not take affirmations from this list and use them as your own. I provide this list only as a reference to give you ideas. If one of these affirmations hits home and you want to use it, change the wording and use it in conjunction with others you come up with.

The safest policy is to use only affirmations that you invent. Those you create will work better for you than those you copy from others. No generic affirmation, even a great and meaningful one, can be as effective as one you devise yourself. Using affirmations you did not formulate does not engage your mind in the same way as using ones you did.

Your affirmations are unique. You are unlike any human being who has ever lived on the face of this planet. Your innermost thoughts and desires are a reflection of you, alone. You are not a generic person.

Moving forward...

You are now ready to create your affirmations. Write all affirmations in the following form:

I, (your name) , (the affirmation) .

Again, make sure each affirmation is (1) specific and (2) positive. Take your time and word them carefully.

The number of affirmations varies from person to person. Most people, after doing this formulation process, end up with somewhere between three and ten affirmations. A good workable number seems to be about five. Many people have only one or two, and that's fine. If you have more than ten, I suggest you reduce the number by retaining only those you feel strongest about.

Do not be afraid to modify your affirmations at any time for any reason. Your goals may change. New interests may pop up from time to time. Things that are important to you now may not be so important later. If you feel like making changes in your affirmations, do so.

At some point in time, you may choose to drop your small-time affirmations and concentrate on your big-timers. Later on, after some of your affirmations have become manifest, you will need to do one of two things: either drop them, or revise them by setting your goals even higher.

If, after a while, one of your affirmations does not feel right, be willing to reword it or drop it. Never resist the inclination to modify or eliminate an affirmation. There is no disgrace in changing your mind. Change is a sign of an evolving consciousness. Some people, after only a few months, have discarded every single one of their original affirmations and created an entire new set. Do not hesitate to make changes, as long as the changes feel right to you. These are *your* affirmations. You can do whatever you want with them, whenever you want to do it.

If this is your first time using affirmations, do not be surprised if you see a need for some modifications after only a few days. In as little as ten days of working with your subconscious mind, your mentality changes. Act accordingly. Revise your affirmations if you feel the inclination to do so. Make sure you are doing exactly what feels right for you at that moment, not what felt right for you last week.

I recommend you reformulate your affirmations on a regular basis. You can do this as often as once a month or as seldom as once a year. Once every three to six months works best for most people. Use the same procedure you just used. Start from scratch; formulate your two lists (your immediate solutions and your ultimate wants); evaluate the items in accordance with the five criteria and retain only those items that pass your scrutiny. Write the remaining items in the form of affirmations. When you perform this reevaluation, some of your previous affirmations remain unchanged and some change only slightly. Often, however, you discover new ones and release ones you no longer care about.

You now have your first list of affirmations. Just for fun, hang on to this list and look back on it a year from now. You will find the list fascinating and informative one year hence. Many people accomplish every one of their initial affirmations within the first year.

You have taken your first step toward success. By formulating your affirmations, you have started doing something about your financial situation, instead of hoping to get around to doing something someday. No more stagnant life for you! You are moving forward now.

Counting to three...

Now that you have your list of affirmations, here's how to get the images implanted into your subconscious mind. Do the following three things every day.

FIRST: Immediately upon awaking in the morning, read your affirmations out loud and visualize them. Take your page of affirmations and, starting at the top, read through the entire list. Read each affirmation clearly. Pronounce every word slowly and distinctly. Be audible and listen to your voice.

Do this soon after waking, when your mind is still impressionable. Shortly after you wake up, your mind enters full waking consciousness and becomes less receptive. The longer you wait, the less effective your reading will be. Try to read your affirmations no later than fifteen minutes after you wake up.

When you say affirmations out loud, your subconscious mind hears your voice speaking. This allows the images to penetrate deeply. Your voice, no matter how it sounds to you or anyone else, is familiar and reassuring to your subconscious mind. When your subconscious mind hears your voice affirm something, it believes what is said. By actually moving your mouth to shape the words, you call upon the muscles and nerve cells of your body to add impulse to the ideas expressed. Do not be afraid to talk out loud in a full speaking voice.

If you live alone, saying your affirmations aloud should be no problem. Leave your list of affirmations beside your bed and, immediately upon waking, roll over, grab the list and read it out loud. If you live with others, however, you may prefer that they do not hear you read. In that case, you need privacy. You may want to read your affirmations where no one can hear you, such as in the bathroom with the door shut. Here's a tip: you can hide the sound of your voice by turning on a radio or television in the same room as the person listening.

If you absolutely cannot arrange to say your affirmations out loud without being heard, then whisper. At the very least, move your lips silently to the formation of each word. The movement of your lips, jaws and tongue—that is, the formation of the words with your mouth—directs the energy to your subconscious mind. Speaking audibly is best, but if you cannot do that, do what you can.

After reading each affirmation, pause a few seconds and visualize an image that relates to what you just said. Form a clear picture in your mind of something that is relevant to your affirmation. Some people refer to this technique as creative visualization.

Creative visualization directs the energy that springs from your desires and adds that energy to your images. This "brands" your images into the "hide" of your mind.

Creative visualization attaches the power
of potential reality to your images.

Visualization is more than casual imagining. Visualization is constructing a detailed and complete image in your mind's eye. When you do creative visualization, you "see" the thing as if it were physically present.

To apply creative visualization, select an image or scenario that aligns with your affirmation. Close your eyes, take a breath and relax into a calm space. Free your mind of clutter. Gently direct your consciousness to the image you want. Allow your mind to observe it. See the picture as if projected onto an imaginary movie screen in your head. Watch and enjoy. Let yourself view the image as it unfolds in dynamic detail.

Suppose you have an affirmation about paying an overdue bill. You might visualize the invoice with a big red "PAID IN FULL" stamped across it. You might see the cancelled check with which you paid the bill. You might imagine a future conversation between you and the creditor in which the two of you joke about that old bill you owed a long time ago.

Let's say you want a new car. Feel your hands on the wheel. Imagine how the stick shift slides into gear. See how the road looks in the rearview mirror. Picture a friend seated next to you as you drive. Imagine washing the car on a summer afternoon.

If you have an affirmation for a new house, visualize the house in detail. Picture the yard and the neighborhood. Imagine mowing the lawn and trimming the shrubs. Envision pulling into the driveway after a day of shopping. Picture walking through the house, room to room. Notice the furniture arrangement. See a party in progress with all your friends whooping it up.

The number of images you can create is infinite. Each time you say an affirmation, your visualization can be different from any previous time. The technique of creative visualization is an opportunity for you to have fun and invent images you like.

In summary, the first daily activity is reading and visualizing each of your current affirmations. Do this immediately after you wake up in the morning. For an average list of five affirmations, this procedure should take approximately one to three minutes.

SECOND: Once during the day, write one of your affirmations repeatedly. You can do this anytime—morning, afternoon or evening—whenever you have a pencil and paper and a few uninterrupted minutes. (Some people ask if they can write their affirmations during the same session when they do their daily reading. The answer is yes, provided the timing is convenient for them. Many people prefer doing it then.)

Pick one of your affirmations. You can choose one that excites you, one you particularly want to work on or one you haven't put much effort into lately. You can pick the same one several days in a row or a different one every time. Once you've made your selection, write the affirmation over and over. You should write it a minimum of ten times. Twenty times is even better. The more times you write an affirmation, the more quickly you see results. Do not overdo it, though. Never write to the point of experiencing writer's cramp. Fifty times, for example, is probably too many.

If you decide to write your affirmation ten to twenty times each day, you will do well. That is a sufficient number of times to get good results. Be flexible though. You can vary the number of times you write an affirmation based on how you feel on any given day. The number of times need not be a hard and fast rule you adhere to without flexibility.

One question I am asked a lot is, "Must I write my affirmations longhand or can I use a word processor?" I recommend longhand. My personal feeling is that a computer is a wonderful tool for many purposes, but it is less than ideal for writing affirmations. The old pen and paper is best. Something about using the muscles of your hand to form the letters of the words plants the message deep in your mind. Nonetheless, some people achieve results from typing. In recent years, I've heard many testimonials from people who use a computer. Apparently, for people who do a lot of typing and are comfortable at the keyboard, doing affirmations that way can work. If you insist, go ahead and try using a word processor. For most people, however, writing longhand works best.

Here are three hints to help you focus attention on what you are writing and plant your images deeply. Follow these suggestions when writing affirmations:

(1) Use a plain, unruled sheet of paper and attempt to make your lines of writing straight and parallel. This improves your sense of order and precision.

(2) Make your writing legible. Although nobody other than you will see what you write, doing this improves your clarity of thought.

(3) Slightly reduce the usual size of your writing. This improves your concentration.

Once in a while, you may also do well to write each affirmation in the first, second and third person, in rotating order. For example:

I, John, own a new red BMW 840.
You, John, own a new red BMW 840.
He, John, owns a new red BMW 840.
I, John, own a new red BMW 840.
•
•
•

Writing in the second and third person can be effective because much of your negative conditioning has come to you from others in this manner. No matter what pronoun you use, though, do not forget to include your name in the affirmation.

A typical writing session should take somewhere between two and ten minutes, depending on your speed and the number of times you write the affirmation. Most people do their writing in five minutes or less.

THIRD: Read your affirmations out loud and briefly visualize each one. This should be the last thing you do before retiring at night. It is an exact repeat of the morning procedure.

Try to do this reading as close as possible to the time you fall asleep. The same considerations apply here as apply to your morning reading. If you sleep alone, you should have no problem reading your affirmations out loud in bed before you doze off. If you sleep with another person, you may prefer to read privately somewhere else in the house before climbing into bed. I leave the details to you.

That's all there is to it. Just read your affirmations morning and night, and write one affirmation sometime during the day. Do these three things every day and you are on your way to reaching your goals.

This three-part procedure requires less than ten minutes per day. It is easy, and it is fun. If you can count to three, you can do it. No matter what you want in life, if you follow these instructions exactly as I've outlined them, you will have it.

Doing it over and over...

Repetition is essential to affirmations. Whatever you repeat, true or false, your subconscious mind comes to believe. Ralph Waldo Emerson said, "A man is what he thinks all day." When you repeat an idea frequently, your subconscious mind accepts the idea as fact and begins the task of converting the idea into reality. Psychologists call this the Law of Predominant Mental Impression.

If, all your life, you tell yourself you cannot accumulate money, you implant that negative image into your subconscious mind. No matter what you try, you are unable to accumulate money. Savings plans, real estate formulas and strategies that work for others somehow fail for you. Your predicament is the product of repeating a negative thought.

The solution is to repeat a suitable affirmation to counter that thought. Say, "I, John, easily accumulate money." With enough repetition, your subconscious mind believes what you tell it. The image of you accumulating money replaces the old image of you struggling to make ends meet. Your subconscious mind then has no choice but to produce the conditions necessary to make your new image a reality.

You must repeat your affirmations over and over, hundreds of times. Eventually, no matter what else you do in your life, you begin to accumulate money. Once your subconscious mind has an image of success, everything happens to support favorable outcomes.

You already possess your fair share of negative images. The negative images are there, and they remain with you until positive images replace them. Unless you deliberately cultivate new images, you will continue on your present course.

DO NOTHING AND NOTHING WILL HAPPEN.

Repeating your affirmations is the most productive thing you can do. Repetition gets to your subconscious mind in a way nothing else can. When you think a particular thought, you start a ball rolling. If you think the thought only once, the ball stops rolling immediately. Nothing materializes as a result of just one thought because insufficient energy is activated to see results. If, however, you repeat the same thought on a regular basis, the ball continues rolling and gathers momentum. Before long, you see results in real life.

What do you think would happen if you said an affirmation only one time and never said it again? Do you suppose you would see any results? Repeat the same affirmation frequently over a period of time, however, and your subconscious mind creates earth-shaking results. Through repetition, the image becomes firmly implanted.

REPETITION OF AN AFFIRMATION
IS THE MOST EFFECTIVE WAY KNOWN
TO VOLUNTARILY DEVELOP AN IMAGE
AT THE SUBCONSCIOUS LEVEL OF MIND.

The first time you say an affirmation, your conscious mind blows the whistle. Your rational mind knows that what you said is not true, and it informs you of your false statement at a high mental volume. If you say the affirmation only once, your conscious mind objects, and that's the end of the matter. In that case, your conscious mind has the last say. But, by repeating the affirmation, *you* have the last say. In that case, the image sneaks past your conscious mind and into your subconscious mind. Repetition renders your conscious mind helpless.

You can observe your inner dialog by writing one of your affirmations over and over for a period of time and listening carefully to your silent mental responses. The dialog that takes place probably looks something like the dialog illustrated below.

AFFIRMATION	MENTAL RESPONSE
I, John, own a red BMW 840.	
I, John, own a red BMW 840.	
I, John, own a red BMW 840.	
I, John, own a red BMW 840.	*No way!*
I, John, own a red BMW 840.	*Don't be ridiculous!*
I, John, own a red BMW 840.	*Who are you trying to kid?*
I, John, own a red BMW 840.	
I, John, own a red BMW 840.	
I, John, own a red BMW 840.	
I, John, own a red BMW 840.	*Bull!*
I, John, own a red BMW 840.	*What a crock!*
I, John, own a red BMW 840.	*Just look out in the driveway.*
I, John, own a red BMW 840.	*See that clunker out there?*
I, John, own a red BMW 840.	*That's what you own!*
I, John, own a red BMW 840.	
I, John, own a red BMW 840.	

I, John, own a red BMW 840.
I, John, own a red BMW 840.   *This garbage won't work.*
I, John, own a red BMW 840.   *I feel ridiculous doing this.*
I, John, own a red BMW 840.   *It won't do any good.*

•

•

•

I, John, own a red BMW 840.
I, John, own a red BMW 840.   *This can't possibly work.*
I, John, own a red BMW 840.   *Can't possibly do anything!*
I, John, own a red BMW 840.   *What a sucker I must be...*
I, John, own a red BMW 840.   *to swallow this nonsense!*
I, John, own a red BMW 840.   *What a jerk!*
I, John, own a red BMW 840.   *What an idiot I am!*
I, John, own a red BMW 840.

•

•

•

I, John, own a red BMW 840.
I, John, own a red BMW 840.   *Doing this is stupid!*
I, John, own a red BMW 840.   *But it probably can't hurt.*
I, John, own a red BMW 840.   *I don't think for a minute...*
I, John, own a red BMW 840.   *I'll get a car from it though.*
I, John, own a red BMW 840.

•

•

•

I, John, own a red BMW 840.
I, John, own a red BMW 840.   *This is an asinine thing.*
I, John, own a red BMW 840.   *This is nuts!*
I, John, own a red BMW 840.   *But it's not too bad doing it.*
I, John, own a red BMW 840.   *Actually, it's not too bad.*
I, John, own a red BMW 840.

I, John, own a red BMW 840.   *I suppose this ain't too bad.*
I, John, own a red BMW 840.   *Kinda funny really.*
I, John, own a red BMW 840.

•

•

•

I, John, own a red BMW 840.
I, John, own a red BMW 840.   *I wish I could believe this.*
I, John, own a red BMW 840.   *It sure would be nice if...*
I, John, own a red BMW 840.
I, John, own a red BMW 840.
I, John, own a red BMW 840.   *New shiny 840!*
I, John, own a red BMW 840.   *Sunroof, whitewalls...*
I, John, own a red BMW 840.
I, John, own a red BMW 840.   *Aw, man! What nonsense!*

•

•

•

I, John, own a red BMW 840.
I, John, own a red BMW 840.   *I have about as much chance...*
I, John, own a red BMW 840.   *of getting a new BMW...*
I, John, own a red BMW 840.   *as...*
I, John, own a red BMW 840.
I, John, own a red BMW 840.   *Sure would be nice though.*
I, John, own a red BMW 840.   *Show it to Kathy...*
I, John, own a red BMW 840.   *She'd be impressed.*
I, John, own a red BMW 840.
I, John, own a red BMW 840.
I, John, own a red BMW 840.   *Not yet though.*
I, John, own a red BMW 840.   *Not just yet.*
I, John, own a red BMW 840.
I, John, own a red BMW 840.   *But maybe someday...*
I, John, own a red BMW 840.   *Hmm, maybe...*

In time, your mental responses mellow. The shift is subtle, and you may need some time to notice. Nonetheless, at some point, you start feeling strangely responsive to the affirmation. Gradually, your inner dialog changes.

•

•

•

I, John, own a red BMW 840.
I, John, own a red BMW 840.   *I can't wait.*
I, John, own a red BMW 840.   *Sure is gonna be great.*
I, John, own a red BMW 840.   *I can see it now!*
I, John, own a red BMW 840.   *I'll get it. I know I will.*
I, John, own a red BMW 840.   *Red and black interior...*
I, John, own a red BMW 840.   *Drive soooooo smooth...*
I, John, own a red BMW 840.   *It won't be long now!*
I, John, own a red BMW 840.   *I'm there, dude!*

Be persistent. Eventually, your mental responses swing to the positive side, especially as your goal draws near. When you finally reach it, look out! Your attitude will be unstoppable. You'll need to drop the affirmation because you will have already achieved it!

How long does it take to see results? Not long. In thirty days or less, you should start to see an indication that something is happening. By that time, you will feel a lot more positive about your prospects for success.

Through repetition, your subconscious mind comes to believe what you are saying. True or false is irrelevant. Even if your statement is false at first, after your mind alters reality, the statement becomes true! If you repeat an outright falsehood many, many times, two things happen: first, your mind accepts the false statement as truth, and second, reality changes so that truth aligns with what was once false. In time, your statement is no longer false, but as true as can be.

Although repetition is important, do not ever write your affirmations to the point of exhaustion. Do not cram hours of effort into one sitting. An energy-draining marathon is counterproductive. A moderate program, like I suggest, done consistently every day, is all you need. The combination of writing and speaking (that is, focussed body movement), applied on a daily basis, implants the images of your choice very effectively. Just keep doing it over and over, and you can't miss.

Committing one hundred percent...

Do your affirmations every day. This is mandatory. No discussion. Do not start missing days and hope it goes unnoticed. Your subconscious mind will know.

If doing affirmations is inconvenient one day, do them anyway. Missing only one day one time takes a huge toll; missing a few days once in a while renders this technique ineffective. There is no room for sloppiness here. Do not skip even one day; the adverse effect is exponential.

A partial effort is of no value. If you intend to give this plan a halfhearted try, you may as well forget the whole thing right now. Don't waste your time. You must commit to this method one hundred percent. Decide to do it, then stay with it every day. Make a solemn pledge to yourself to give this plan your undying devotion.

I designed a performance chart for you. This is the same chart I, myself, use and give to others. It is printed on the following page. Feel free to enlarge it and reproduce it for your own use. (If you prefer, you can obtain a full-size version that is easier to make copies from. Refer to the Personal Power Pack, Appendix C, page 265.)

PERSONAL PERFORMANCE CHART

Name: _____ Month: _____ Year: _____

DAILY ACTIVITIES

FIRST: Morning Reading & Visualization
SECOND: Writing (one affirmation only)
THIRD: Evening Reading & Visualization

Day	FIRST	SECOND	THIRD	Comments
1				
2				
3				
4				
5				
6				
7				
8				
9				
10				
11				
12				
13				
14				
15				
16				
17				
18				
19				
20				
21				
22				
23				
24				
25				
26				
27				
28				
29				
30				
31				

Comments: _____
_____

This chart helps you stick to a schedule and stay with your program. It also ensures that you do not skip any part of the daily three-part procedure.

Keep your chart somewhere easily accessible and in plain view. Tack it to a wall, set it next to your bed or put it anywhere you can see it. Keep a pen or pencil nearby.

To use the chart, place a check mark in the appropriate space after you complete that activity. In the second column, you may wish to include a notation indicating which affirmation you wrote that day and how many times you wrote it. The object is to mark all three columns for every day of the month.

The space at the bottom is for monthly comments. Record any noticeable results, including positive events and improvements that happen during the month. You can also include a comment expressing how you feel about your progress for the month. If you need more room, write on the back.

At the end of each month, examine your performance. Does every space contain a check mark? If so, congratulate yourself. If not, give yourself a good talking-to. If you see a large number of blank spaces, do not get discouraged and abandon your program in defeat. Make an agreement with yourself to do better next month. If you honestly were unable to complete the three parts every day, do not beat yourself up about it. Do the best you can each month and let it go at that. But remember, even an occasional miss can nullify results. For this reason, total commitment is essential.

Save your charts. You will find your comments useful to look back on later. And by saving these charts, you have an overview of how you are doing and what's been happening in your life.

Keeping faith...

Here are three additional ways to use your affirmations. Although these techniques are not required, they can be enjoyable and can strengthen your resolve. You can do all of them or none of them, occasionally or never. You decide if and when to add them to your regimen.

(1) Look at yourself in a mirror while saying your affirmations. Gaze directly into your eyes and say each affirmation clearly and audibly. This technique focuses the energy generated by your images and directs it at your subconscious mind.

(2) Record your affirmations on a cassette tape and play them back. (An endless-loop tape works well for this.) First, repeat your affirmations enough times to fill the tape. Then, play them back and listen. Play them in your car while driving. Play them on your walkman while jogging. Play them at home while lying in bed. If you doze off while listening, the power of autosuggestion continues to work while you sleep. Most people find this technique relaxing and reassuring.

(3) Write a few affirmations on individual index cards and carry them with you during the day. Every once in a while, when you feel stressed or bothered, pull out a card and read it a few times. This technique serves a dual purpose: it reinforces the affirmation, and it immediately makes you feel calm and centered.

I knew a woman who felt upset and irritable nearly all the time. She claimed her job was to blame. Her boss was an unreasonable man, and he showed her no mercy. The stress she felt did not subside when she arrived home at night. All evening long, she was restless and short-tempered. Her relationship with her young son began to deteriorate. Everything was falling apart for her. She felt her life going down the drain.

One day, she started carrying an affirmation on a little card. Whenever a tense moment came up at work, she secluded herself in the bathroom, pulled out the card and repeated the affirmation to herself. The affirmation did not pertain to her job; it was an affirmation for a piece of antique furniture she wanted.

Whenever the woman did this, she immediately felt better. She would find a smile creeping across her face, even if only at the thought of how ridiculous this technique was. A few moments later, she was feeling relaxed and cheerful. Reading the affirmation helped her regain confidence and keep faith in her abilities. When she walked back into the office, she carried with her an air of self-assurance. Others sensed her new attitude.

Within weeks, her outlook on life changed. She became less irritable away from work, as her job-related problems stayed at the office. She enjoyed her time at home, and her relationship with her son blossomed. All this, mind you, was accomplished by reading an affirmation having nothing to do with the specific problem.

Now, a little more than one year later, this woman is self-employed with a profitable business of her own; she and her son get along wonderfully; and her home is full of antique furniture.

Staying mute...

I recommend that you do not tell anyone about your affirmations. This advice may sound harsh, but I assure you, there is a good reason for it.

The reason to keep quiet is *not* to promote mystery or to satisfy some inane craving for suspense. The reason is simply that silence works best. Keeping silent is not required—you can share your program with your spouse or the whole world for that matter—but those who maintain silence show a far better record of success.

My advice is to not tell anyone about your new program or even that there *is* a new program. Silence is especially important at the beginning. Your attitude when you start is particularly vulnerable, since you have not yet begun to experience the onslaught of good fortune that comes later.

Most people, when they hear about your program, say something critical. They mean well; they just don't understand the effect their comment has. They are not malicious people. In all likelihood, they are sincerely trying to be helpful. Perhaps, they are just making conversation. But a questionable comment can hit hard and deflate your motivation. For example:

"Sounds like one of those positive thinking deals."

"Doesn't seem very logical."

"Strikes me as kinda weird...but whatever."

"Hmmm, You're actually doing this stuff?"

"My aunt tried some plan from a book one time, and it didn't work." (Well, so much for Auntie!)

Even innocent comments like these can have a devastating effect on your enthusiasm. They are ordinary remarks, but deadly.

When you are beginning this method, you are not yet convinced that it works. You may be testing the technique to see what happens. An ill-informed comment is the last thing you need to hear. Regardless of your initial level of determination, the slightest hint of negativity can infect you with doubt and send you scurrying to the safety of inactivity. Believe me on this point, the majority of well-meaning people say something critical when they find out what you're up to.

Another reason for you to keep silent is that secrecy conserves your power of creative thought. Telling others expends that power. You suffer a psychic loss of energy in the process of informing others of expected changes. Such an announcement calls attention to what you are doing and creates undue pressure by putting you on the spot. If results require more time than you anticipate, your friends might remind you how long the process is taking. These are comments you can do without. Even if the people you want to tell are accepting and supportive individuals, do not discuss your program with them.

"Be silent and safe—silence never betrays you."
John Boyle O'Reilly

You might need a dose of ingenuity to keep your plan secret from family members and those close to you. (You may even want to hide this book from them, at least for a while.) Do whatever you must. If you try, I'm sure you can pull it off.

Before long, your life will start changing. Everything you touch will turn to gold. Once that starts happening, people will notice. Results will be obvious to those around you. You will not need to broadcast that something is different. People will come to you and ask what's happening. They'll want to know if you are practicing some secret formula for success. Smile. Go ahead and tell whomever you want then. You'll get no arguments.

You may not agree with my advice right now. You may think this advice is extreme. You may think, in your case, telling someone would be okay. You may think that your "someone" is special and that sharing your secret would be acceptable. Whatever you think, don't tell. I urge you to stay mute on the subject. Believe me, I have seen the most determined individuals abandon their efforts prematurely because they thought they could tell a special someone. Don't leave your mind vulnerable to negative influences from others. It's your decision, but that is my advice.

Tending tomatoes...

So, there you have it. You now know how to formulate affirmations and what to do with them. You know everything necessary to put this plan into action. You have at your command a foolproof way to implant the images of your choice into your subconscious mind. You are one fortunate individual.

"Only the dreamer can change the dream."
John Logan

You do not need to understand how this procedure works to use it. I gave you a little background information, but if you did not grasp it, don't worry. If you cannot fathom the stuff about quantum physics or mind dynamics, don't sweat it. You do not need to know any of that.

Nobody invented electricity. It has always been here. Ben Franklin merely *discovered* electricity. Since that time, we have learned how to make effective use of his discovery by harnessing electricity to serve our needs.

Today, anyone can go to the wall, flip on the switch, and presto—a miracle. The room fills with light. You do not need to understand the nature of electricity in order to use it. In fact, not one person alive, even today, knows exactly what electricity is. With all our knowledge, electricity remains a mystery.

The subconscious mind, with its ability to restructure reality, is much like electricity. It is a natural phenomenon. Nobody invented it, and nobody knows exactly how it works. Nonetheless, anyone can put it to use.

By repeating your affirmations, you are using the power of your subconscious mind as easily as a nursery school child uses electricity by turning on a light. If you don't know tiddly-toot about how it works, so what.

Do not let any lack of technical understanding deter you from doing your affirmations. You don't let your limited knowledge of electromagnetic wave theory deter you from turning on the television set when you want to watch your favorite show, do you? You don't let your weak grasp of aerodynamics prevent you from hopping on an airplane, do you? You don't let your ignorance of cellular biology keep you from tending your tomatoes, do you? Of course not.

To grow tomatoes, you plant the seeds in the ground. Once planted, the seeds sprout and grow. You need not worry about the biological processes that make the plant grow. The plant knows exactly how to grow and produce tomatoes. You can trust the plant to do that correctly.

Your subconscious mind knows exactly how to restructure reality. You can trust it. You cannot explain how it works, and you don't need to. All you need to do is read and write your affirmations and trust your subconscious mind do the rest. It will.

Showing fortitude...

Results need time. Do not presume that your affirmations will manifest immediately; sufficient time must pass first. The day will come when your affirmations materialize, but that day happens only after a while. Be patient. Results will appear, but not overnight.

> *"No great thing is created suddenly, any more than a bunch of grapes or a fig. If you tell me that you desire a fig, I answer you that there must be time. Let it first blossom, then bear fruit, then ripen."*
> Epictetus

For many years, you have been reinforcing negative expectations. A long time was needed to solidify these images. Now, patience is in order. You are reversing the pattern of a lifetime. Allow some time. Do not demand too much too soon. Changes will come when they should.

Realize that, however long this process takes, it definitely takes less time than anything else you could do. In as little as ten to thirty days, you could start to see an indication of change, evidence you are headed in the right direction. Certainly, within three months, you should notice some concrete results. I dare say, three months of doing affirmations is not an extreme burden.

> *"If you would one day renovate yourself, do so from day to day."*
> Confucius

Sometimes when I give a lecture on affirmations, a few members of the audience snicker and laugh among themselves. I overhear phrases like "hocus-pocus" and "superstitious nonsense." Personally, I am not bothered in the slightest by these remarks. The skepticism of these people cannot harm me or the effectiveness of affirmations one bit. The lives of countless individuals have proven, beyond any doubt, that affirmations work. No matter how many people scoff, nothing can change that track record.

What does bother me is that such attitudes are preventing these individuals from giving this technique a try. These people have become caught up in their own close-mindedness, trapped by their own unfounded opinions. They remain stuck, unable to bend. Too bad. These folks are limiting their chances for the success that obviously eludes them. I sincerely hope you do not fall into this pitiful category.

Have the strength to shun any ignorant sarcasm you hear around you. Stand up and show the fortitude to think for yourself. If something in these pages strikes you as plausible, then give this method a try. The method can work for you only if you let it.

> *"Failure is not the only punishment for laziness; there's also the success of others."*
> Jules Renard

Many people are reading this book at the same time you are. Those who act on this information will embark on a new path. A few months from now, they will be on their way to a life of prosperity and happiness. Those who talk themselves out of doing anything, will remain exactly where they are. A few months from now, they will still be struggling and dissatisfied. To which group do you belong?

Telling success stories...

On a day in February, several years ago, I moved to San Jose, California. At that point in time, I was an unemployed radio announcer. My work record showed a number of short stints with radio stations around the country, but nothing impressive and nothing in the preceding four years.

Radio is a business that requires proper experience for advancement. An announcer becomes employable only after sufficient years of appropriate training. Or so they say. My hodgepodge work record gave me almost no chance for a decent job. A radio analyst told me I was nuts to try for a spot in a major market.

The first thing I did upon arriving in San Jose was scan the radio dial and listen to every local station, AM and FM. I selected the one I liked best. I decided I wanted to be news director and conduct a telephone-talk show at that station. I walked in off the street and, with my best positive attitude, told them to hire me. The program manager promptly informed me that they had nothing available, and even if they did, they would not be the least bit interested in me. I went home.

By all logical reasoning, I should have concluded that my chance of being hired at that station was zero. The station had no openings, and even if something became available, they would not consider me for the job. My only radio experience was as a disc-jockey, and I hadn't done any radio at all in over four years. I never did news in my life, and I was asking the number-one-rated radio station in a top market to hire me as their news director and give me a talk show!

Not to be discouraged, I started writing affirmations. My affirmations proclaimed that I was news director at that station and had a talk show. I visualized both. I imagined every detail of my radio career. I daydreamed of various on-the-air scenarios. All my thoughts and actions suggested I was already employed as news director and already had the talk show. To even consider that such was not the case seemed to me like some fluke error, some aberration of reality. The idea of me not being news director ran contrary to everything I thought and did in life. I persisted with affirmations. I left the creative powers no other option than to manifest my images.

At the end of March, a position as announcer opened up at the station. I called and stopped by a few times. On April 6th, I was hired. About six weeks later, I was appointed news director. A few weeks after that, I began my regularly-scheduled talk program.

My telephone-talk show soared in ratings to become the most popular program in the area. I conducted the same show—same time, same station—for over six years. That radio program brought me immeasurable satisfaction for a long time. I would not trade the experience of that show for all the money in the world.

What was my likelihood of being hired by that station? Slim. Yet I was hired in less than two months. Unlikely? Yes. But it happened anyway. Logical reasoning holds no candle to the power of your subconscious mind. No matter what the odds, you can buck them with affirmations. I have used affirmations many, many times during my life. Every time, without exception, I have achieved my goal—usually sooner than I expected.

A few years ago, I counseled a woman in her early twenties. She was very unhappy with her life. She worked as a cocktail waitress and hated her job. The first thing I did was ask her, "What do you want?" She had no idea.

I helped her answer that question. I instructed her in the same procedure I outlined for you earlier. Her self-analysis soon uncovered that she loved animals and had always wanted to be a veterinarian. She had suppressed that desire because her rational mind supplied her with negative thoughts on the matter, thoughts like: *I have no training*, *I'm too inept* and *I'm getting too old*. These negative beliefs were preventing her from pursuing what she wanted.

I started her on a program of affirmations. At first, she felt foolish writing, "I, Susan, involve myself every day in the welfare of animals." But she stayed with the program. A few weeks later, she met a man at a party. He was a veterinarian. They dated and fell in love. About six weeks later, the man's office assistant quit her job. He hired Susan as his new helper.

Her life changed quickly from that point on. With this man's coaching and support, she decided to attend school. The last I heard from her, she was studying veterinary medicine and working part-time as an assistant for her husband. Was I surprised? Not at all. With the power of your subconscious mind, anything is possible.

One day, a man came to me in tears. He had lost his job at a bank and was being investigated for embezzlement. I saw panic in his face. He felt he would never again secure a decent job. He was accustomed to a high standard of living, and he was down to about $400 cash to his name. The pressure on this man was unbearable. All he could see in his future was obstacles. He felt his situation was hopeless. By the time he asked my advice, he was considering suicide.

Working together, we uncovered what he wanted. All he cared about was money. He wanted to be filthy rich.

This was a sincere desire for him. He had lived in denial of this desire for years because he figured such a craving must be evil and selfish. But, once he got in touch with his feelings, he admitted this was what he wanted above all else. I did not pass judgment on him. I simply told him what to do to make his desire a reality. He formulated a few affirmations and followed my instructions.

Shortly thereafter, the real bank embezzler was apprehended. My friend moved to New York City and became a stock broker. I heard from him recently. He informed me that his net worth had grown to over two million dollars. He had met the woman of his dreams and together they were moving to a property in Idaho. He told me money was no longer a focus for him. He had attained financial independence and now intended to enjoy life to its fullest—as a rancher! He was so excited about the future he could hardly contain himself.

Whatever you affirm, no matter what it is, will be realized. In the case I just cited, the man wanted money. I allowed him to feel alright about that desire. I did not judge him. Once he achieved his monetary goal, he was then free to reexamine his life and discover what he wanted at a deeper level. His desires changed, and that's normal. Whatever you want, whatever comes up for you as a unique individual, that's alright. Don't deny it. Accept it and go for it. And feel good about it. Always strive for what you want at that moment. Whatever it is, it's okay. And whatever it is, you can have it.

I once interviewed a woman who told me she wanted men to call her on the telephone. Sounds trivial, perhaps, but it was a strong desire for her at that point in her life. She wanted this more than anything. Once she knew her desire, she started writing affirmations to bring it about. Sure, at first she thought this procedure was silly; but she wanted phone calls so badly she was willing to try almost anything. Her affirmation said, "I, Sondra, now receive an abundance of calls from men on my home telephone." She found it easy to imagine her phone ringing; her visualizations were strong and vivid.

Four days later, she was bubbling with joy. Men whom she had not heard from in years were calling her out of the blue. Old lovers unexpectedly decided to phone. Men at work asked for her number and were calling. She even received several wrong numbers in the middle of the night—from men. I do not suggest her desire represents the highest of ambitions, but her story illustrates that whatever you properly program into your subconscious mind comes to pass. By the way, since that time, she has been applying her affirmations to other, more productive, areas of her life.

A boy of sixteen had worked himself into a frenzy. He feared he would grow too big. In the past year, his body had shot to 6'2" tall, and his shoe size was over 14. Both were increasing rapidly and showed no signs of slowing. He feared he would become a giant. When the shoe salesperson measured his foot at size 15, he knew something had to be done.

I instructed him in the use of affirmations. At first, the object was to stop the rate of growth, to hold steady. He wrote affirmations saying he was 6'2" tall, and had a foot size of 14. Immediately, his body stopped growing. A year went by. Overwhelmed with this miracle, he decided to go further. He wrote an affirmation for a size 13 foot. The most recent measurement, done in a shoe store, showed his foot size at exactly 13. By using affirmations, he had reduced the size of his feet.

With affirmations, you can do anything. The sky is the limit. Here are a few things for which I have personally seen people use affirmations:

Pay overdue bills.
Own a beautiful house.
Eliminate wrinkles and look younger.
Get a pilot's license.
Improve eyesight.
Become famous and popular.
Increase sales.
Have lots of lovers.
Improve athletic skill.
Win at poker.
Find items in a scavenger hunt.
Lose weight and keep it off.
Acquire merchandise.
Succeed at business.
Regain the use of a paralyzed limb.
Secure a high-paying job.
Halt the spread of a malignant tumor.
Locate a long-lost relative.
Improve sexual functioning.
Become wealthy.
Overcome a fear of water.
Attract a marriage partner.
Excel at bodybuilding and weight lifting.
Improve the rhythm of a golf swing.
Pay for college tuition and board.
Invent new and useful products.
Be a rock n' roll star.
Score more touchdowns.
Get out of jail.
Increase physical endurance.

Catch bigger fish.
Win contests and sweepstakes.
Improve personal relationships.
Become more confident.
Play tennis better.
Grow a healthier garden.
Find the car keys.
Strengthen arm and back muscles.
Eliminate recurring herpes.
Climb to the top of a mountain.
Learn a new trade.
Stop smoking and drinking.
Raise well-mannered children.
Make grocery money go further.
Gain more respect from colleagues.
Throw better curve balls.
Reduce stuttering and speech problems.
Overcome blocks to creativity.
Communicate more effectively.
House-train pets.
Improve gas mileage.

People of all ages, all races and all persuasions are using affirmations to achieve their unique goals. No matter what you want, affirmations are a way to get it.

"I don't want to know the odds!"
Han Solo, in *Star Wars*

I did not include personal success stories in this book to blow your mind. The ones I selected are not even the most shocking. By comparison, they are rather typical. But they illustrate the manner in which affirmations work. And I enjoy telling stories like these.

I'm sure you've heard success stories before. So have I. I've heard thousands. Some are astounding. Big deal. Somebody else's success story probably means little to you. I understand. You need something more tangible, · something you can touch, something that's yours. So, why not create a little success story of your own?

Changing lives...

Are you happy with your life right now? Are you truly satisfied? How about finances? Are you confident that you will always have money when you need it? Are you comfortable with every aspect of your life? If not, that's good. That gives you something to work with.

Next question: Are you ready for change? Don't just say yes out of reflex. You must *feel* ready—deep inside your heart. You must be sick and tired, fed up with the way things are. You must yearn for change. Above all, you must be willing to do something about it. Only when you are prepared to act, can you say you are ready. If you are ready to do something about your situation, then— and only then—are you honestly ready for change.

> *"Even if you're on the right track, you'll get run over if you just sit there."*
> Will Rogers

Make no mistake about it, most people are not ready for a significant degree of change in their life. They like being poor and miserable. Oh, they may complain often enough. They may gripe and moan about how terrible everything is. But they are not honestly ready to change. Do you know how to tell? Give them something they can do to better their plight, and they will forever make up excuses why they cannot do it. In other words, they are not willing to do anything about their situation. Thus, they are not sincerely ready for change. Are you? Answer honestly. Are you ready to do something about your life?

"Take time to deliberate; but when the time for action arrives, stop thinking and go in."
Andrew Jackson

If you sincerely feel that now is the time for change in your life, then jump aboard this caravan on its way to the top. Right now! This exact moment! Make up your mind to begin now, even as you are reading this.

START NOW! TODAY!

For a long time, you have cultivated negative images of how life should be. Do you like those images? Do you like what they've wrought? Tell the truth. Are you pleased with them? If not, kick them out. Get rid of those tired images, as you would throw out the garbage after dinner. They've outlived their usefulness and overstayed their visit. Kiss them good-bye. How do you do that? I've shown you how—with daily affirmations.

This is the secret you've been waiting for all your life. Follow my instructions, no matter how ridiculous or impractical they seem at first. And then wait. Before long, the blessings of prosperity will be upon you.

CAN YOU RECOGNIZE A SLEEPING GIANT WHEN YOU SEE ONE?

When you read and write affirmations, you remove negative, destructive images that have lived within you, and you replace them with positive, constructive images that endure from this day forth. Your affirmations eliminate any financial problems you now have and replace those problems with the prospect of financial security far into the future.

I want you to feel a little discontent right now—not unhappy or frustrated, but excitedly dissatisfied with things as they are. Only then will you yearn to make things better. I want you to make things better. I want you to create a life for yourself based on the way things *should* be, the way things *can* be—the way things *will* be! I want you to change your life.

> *"Do it! I say. Whatever you want to do, do it now! There are only so many tomorrows."*
> Michael Landon

You've waited long enough to taste wealth and prosperity. Do not wait any longer. For goodness sakes, stop wasting your precious life. Begin now! Kick yourself in the butt and go.

6

Your Life
of Prosperity

THIS CHAPTER CONTAINS extra pointers to maximize your attractive force. They are optional; you do not need to use them. If you do only affirmations and nothing more, you'll still increase the attractive force you generate toward money. However, if you decide to take any of these additional suggestions, results will happen sooner. Don't misunderstand me; I do not mean to overburden you with more things to do. But I want you to have these extra tips to enhance your life of prosperity.

Act the part.

Speech and thought have a strong connection. Most people agree that their speech can influence the thoughts of others. Not many people realize, however, that their speech can influence their own thinking. They should. What you say influences what you think. This influence often extends to the subconscious level. Changing how you talk changes how you think.

Give up your bellyaching. I know complaining can be fun sometimes, but I urge you to let go of it. Believe me, success is far more fun than any shallow enjoyment you gather from wallowing in self-pity. I know, because I've tried both.

If you habitually complain about your financial situation, turn over a new leaf right now. Don't talk about how broke you are. Instead, let your words reinforce that finances are improving for you. For example, when you plan a trip to the theater with some friends, don't mention that you can hardly afford it. Tell everyone cost is no problem.

Do not gripe about expenses. Do not whine about difficulties. Do not expound on encounters with bad luck. You may experience a negative feeling from time to time. That's understandable. But do not magnify the negativity and plant it more deeply in your mind by putting the feeling into words and talking about it.

Eliminate negative statements, such as: *I never had a chance. I didn't go to college. I'm getting old. I have more bad luck than others. I'm stuck in a rut and can't get out. I'm not as smart as I used to be. My family ties me down. People are prejudiced against me. My health is terrible. I don't have enough time. Life is unfair.*

These assertions keep you poor and miserable by reinforcing defeatist attitudes. At best, these statements serve only as excuses. You must stop this type of chatter. Do not talk or act—or even think—in any manner other than prosperously.

Do not get involved when others talk of hard times. Just listen. Be aware that these unhappy people no longer speak your language. Do not accompany them in their pitiful song. If you feel that their complaining is starting to influence you, declare silently to yourself something like, "I am no longer in the same boat with these people. I am on the road to success." In the long run, you'll find the road easier to travel if you associate with confident, productive people.

Let's suppose you and a few friends start a diet together. When you see them, don't say, "This diet is the hardest thing I've ever done." You might think that this type of talk puts you on their good side. Maybe it does. But your negative statements defeat your efforts.

Instead say, "This diet is great. It's working wonders for me. I'm getting thin." Even if you have not lost a pound, talk as though you have. With your new attitude, you might even look thinner to them.

Act and speak as though you have already solved your financial problems, even if no results are apparent yet. Your speech should support the images you are implanting with your affirmations. If you read and write your affirmations every day, but continue to act as though you are broke, results—although inevitable—come later rather than sooner. You want results as soon as possible, right? Then start acting successful, even if your behavior is "all show" at first. Soon, you'll get the results to back up your behavior. Then, you'll no longer be acting. After that, when you go out with a friend and say, "I'll treat, I can afford it," you'll be telling the truth!

Act confident. Don't worry about faking it; a well-acted imitation gets you by until success comes along and makes you genuinely confident.

Act the way you eventually want to be. If you want to be rich, act as though you already are. Behavior reaches your subconscious mind and makes an imprint. Your subconscious mind easily falls for the act because it has no reasoning power. As you continue to act the part, you find that pretending gets increasingly easy. Other people see you as the person you present to them. Eventually, you become that person in reality.

When National City Bank president Frank A. Vanderlip was a child, he asked a wealthy acquaintance for advice on how to succeed in life. The person replied, "Look as though you already have succeeded." In the words of William Shakespeare, "Assume a virtue if you have it not." Act and talk as though you've already achieved your goals. Before long, you will.

Allow daydreams.

From the time we were children, most of us have been told that daydreams are an unproductive waste of time. That is far from true. Daydreams are a direct link to the subconscious mind.

Daydreams surface involuntarily from time to time. Allow them to do so. Cultivate them. Enjoy them. Be grateful for them.

When you encourage daydreams, you find yourself daydreaming more frequently, particularly about your affirmations. That is good. These little scenarios serve as valuable visualizations. Daydreams should never be inhibited or interrupted. When one comes, let it happen. Get into it. Relish it while it lasts. There is little else you could be doing that is more productive.

A good mental exercise is to imagine you've just been handed one million dollars to do with as you please. What would you do? How would you spend it? Have fun with this idea. Do not think a daydream is foolish. Do not be embarrassed by what you daydream. View a daydream as a small step toward making your dreams come true.

Daydreams can occur while sipping tea, resting in bed, waiting for a subway or almost anytime. Allow the imaginary story to progress. See yourself working your ideal job, building your dream house, persuading world leaders, rescuing a princess, meeting Prince Charming or whatever. A daydream is a precious gift. When the daydream ends, you have plenty of time to get back to your regular life. In the meantime, enjoy the show.

Watch for luck-lines.

When you implant an image, your subconscious mind must find a way to materialize that image. Sometimes, your mind employs a strategy that seems strange and unexpected. Often as not, the strategy involves a few luck-lines.

A luck-line is any exposure to a person, place or thing that furthers the realization of your image. Solutions to problems often come to you by means of luck-lines. You can speed things up by watching for these luck-lines.

The mind works in strange ways. Once your mind gets busy restructuring reality, there is no telling how it might carry out its task. Your subconscious mind succeeds no matter what needs to be done.

Once your image is implanted, your mind sets into motion subtle forces that align you with the flow of relevant energy. When this happens, all objects and circumstances appear strangely influenced in a way that brings you closer to your goal. You feel mysteriously drawn toward helpful situations. Be alert to these situations. Watch for them. There is no element of chance involved here. Your life unfolds as it should. Sometimes, these situations are thrust upon you with such immediacy you could not ignore them if you tried. Be ready.

If you implant images designed to attract wealth, situations that relate to wealth come into your life. You suddenly get a tip on a hot investment opportunity. You mysteriously find yourself among wealthy people talking about new ideas. A distant relative offers to fly you across the country to discuss a financial matter. This phenomenon can start slowly at first and speed up later.

Don't be afraid to make new acquaintances. You never know when a seemingly unimportant encounter might lead to the resolution of some issue in your life. The benefit a person can provide to you might be unrelated to the context of your relationship with that person.

A friend of mine, Alice, worked as a nurse at a large urban hospital. On her floor was an elderly woman who had been diagnosed as terminally ill. Alice was kind and receptive to this woman. The sick woman confided in Alice, and Alice responded with friendship and understanding. Alice had no ulterior motive for giving extra attention to this woman; Alice had no idea that this person possessed wealth and influence.

The woman made an unexpected recovery. She attributed her healing, in part, to the love and caring she had received from Alice. Later, she hired Alice as her personal secretary at more than twice the salary Alice had earned at the hospital. With the financial backing and political influence of her new friend, Alice is presently running for city council.

Now, here's the amazing thing: About ten days before Alice met the woman patient at the hospital, Alice realized she was unhappy in the nursing profession. She wanted to get into politics. Although a political career seemed unlikely to her at the time, she wrote an appropriate affirmation anyway.

As you can see, Alice was wise to watch for luck-lines. The woman patient turned out to be just that; she represented a luck-line for Alice. Although Alice could not have known at the time, the sick woman became the critical link to her new future.

Every person who comes into your life is potentially an important contact. When you're doing affirmations, be receptive to all people who enter your life, no matter what the context. Everything that happens has a purpose, even if that purpose is shielded from view. You never know who will turn out to be a vital cog in the machinery of your new life.

Once your subconscious mind springs into action, you meet exactly the right people to assist you in realizing your goals. The people who come into your life supply you with needed help, guidance or information. Sometimes, without the speaker even knowing, an offhand remark tips you off about something important. This may sound astonishing, but major developments often begin in unassuming ways. I've witnessed the power of humble beginnings more times than I can count.

All you need to do is watch for these contacts and be responsive to them when they appear. Pay attention to what is happening around you. Stay alert. Keep a sharp eye peeled for your luck-lines. They'll be coming your way soon.

Cancel unwanted images.

Some negative thoughts are inescapable. No matter what you do, unwanted images creep into your conscious mind once in a while.

Most people freak out when they experience a negative thought. When they realize they are having a bad thought, they panic and try to expel the thought as quickly as possible. That is not the best way to handle unwanted images.

Suppression is never good. Trying to prevent a negative thought from entering your consciousness promotes stress and drains your vital energy. Don't bother. Your attempts fail anyway. If I say to you, "Do not think of a pink elephant," what do you immediately think of? A pink elephant, of course. By attempting to eliminate any occurrence of negative thoughts, the thoughts grow stronger. Trying to suppress unwanted thoughts not only saps your energy but increases the likelihood of having the thoughts in the first place.

Obviously, you do not want these negative thoughts to have an impact on your subconscious mind. So, what should you do? I'll tell you what to do. Use a two-word phrase to cancel the impact of your negative thoughts. The magic phrase is:

"Cancel. Cancel."

First of all, whenever you find yourself immersed in an unwanted thought, don't worry about it. Do not suppress it. Let the thought happen. Immediately after the thought fades, say to yourself, "Cancel, Cancel." This phrase nullifies any effect the thought might have on your subconscious mind.

If you suddenly become aware you are having an unwanted visualization, do not be concerned. You might be sitting at home daydreaming when, all of a sudden, you realize you are vividly imagining some horrible series of events. Let the scenario come to its natural conclusion, then say to yourself, "Cancel, Cancel." This technique prevents otherwise destructive visualizations from exerting influence on your subconscious mind. Let this phrase become your natural response to unwanted thoughts.

You may be driving in your car, and you imagine the vehicle flying over a cliff. You may be visiting a friend, and you picture him picking up a scissors and trying to stab you. You may be walking the dog, and you see yourself being tortured in a prison cell. You may be reviewing some figures with your spreadsheet, and you visualize the failure of your new business. Thoughts like these are uninvited and unwanted, but, like it or not, they happen anyway.

Unwanted thoughts are common. They do not mean you are sick or perverted. In confidential surveys, a majority of people report having unwanted visualizations, some quite bizarre.

No matter how clear or powerful these visualizations are, you can keep them from having a subconscious effect by using the phrase I just gave you. Allow the visualization, horrible though it may be, to progress to its logical conclusion. Then say to yourself, "Cancel, Cancel." Then relax, confident in the knowledge that any negative effect has been squelched.

This secret phrase is now being taught in numerous self-improvement seminars around the world. These seminars range in price from $100 to $3000. For those willing to use it, this two-word phrase is a steal, even at that price. Try it, you'll like it.

Learn from experience.

Charles Schwab made well over 100 million dollars in his lifetime. He once said, "I have failed forty-nine percent of the time and succeeded only fifty-one percent of the time." Obviously, this two-percent difference is a critical margin.

When events do not unfold the way you want, do not dwell on it. Get on with your life, and keep trying. Life is constructed so that you win some and you lose some. That's just the way it is. Accept it. If you manage to win slightly more often than you lose—although you may still lose plenty—you'll be in good shape.

You will encounter situations that do not go your way. The problem comes when you interpret those situations as final. If you are driving to a party and take a wrong turn, should you give up? Of course, not. If you are wise, you simply turn around and learn from your mistake.

No one experiences continual, uninterrupted progress in any aspect of life. The road to success is littered with setbacks. Progress always occurs in stages, with periods of difficulty mixed in. You might be making huge strides, and, all of a sudden, the roof caves in. That can happen. You need to accept mishaps as part of the overall flow. If you read the biographies of successful men and women, you find they all made mistakes, endured delays and suffered setbacks. But they learned something along the way. Whatever happens to you on your journey to success, try to learn something from it.

Cultivate courage.

People fear many things. They fear poverty, criticism, ill-health, lost love, old age and the creeping hand of death. Fear inhibits your ability to reason effectively. It paralyzes your imagination. It discourages initiative and undermines enthusiasm. Fear slows your migration toward success. From now on, allow fear to fall by the wayside. You have no further use for it.

Reach out and do what you are inspired to do. There is a reason for that inspiration; act on it. Follow your hunches. Remember, you will make some mistakes. Don't be afraid of them. Mistakes are part of life. So who cares! Go ahead and take a chance. If you goof up, that's okay. If you succeed, however, then you've got something. This much is certain: you will never succeed if you do not try. Don't worry about failure. You'll succeed often enough.

Have confidence in yourself. With a few successes under your belt, you'll find it easy to be optimistic and self-assured. Get on this cycle:

Have courage. Do not be frightened by the prospect of botching things up. Try and try again. You are building a new life for yourself, a life free from the fear that haunts you now. A little courage puts you on the right track. Go for it.

Integrate all feelings.

Suppression is the act of forcing a thought or feeling out of your conscious mind. Suppression leaves you in a state of denial, refusing to see what is real. The problem with suppression is that feelings you attempt to hide get sent down to your subconscious mind. There, they continue to do their dirty work influencing your life.

People suppress a feeling when the feeling is unpleasant and they prefer not to feel it at that moment. But this approach does not get rid of the feeling. Suppression merely causes the feeling to be stored subconsciously instead of consciously. Suppressed feelings are stored physically as a pattern of energy in the cells of your body. These patterns remain for years, contributing to stress and accelerating symptoms of old age.

Suppressed feelings slow the process of implanting new images. Since these feelings are stored in your subconscious mind, the task of countering them takes longer than if the feelings were not suppressed to begin with.

Integration is the opposite of suppression. Integration releases suppressed feelings and frees you from the burdens they impose. The process of integration is the process of coming out of denial, of accepting buried feelings and experiencing them in detail. Once you experience a feeling for what it is, all negativity associated with that feeling evaporates. Integration is a pleasurable process that leaves you free and empowered.

Many techniques exist to help you integrate your feelings. Breathwork and meditation can be helpful tools. Explore some of these methods concurrently with your program of affirmations. Integrating feelings speeds the results of your affirmations by inviting the needed changes into your life.

Stay receptive to love.

The basic human need for love and affection is an important element in the formula for success. Your yearning for intimacy is maintained by the same forces that create reality from ideas. An instinct for love is a direct function of energy. The excitement of sex, the exhilaration of a newfound romance and the joy of a well-matched relationship all contribute to your sense of worth, which, in turn, contributes to your ability to succeed and prosper.

Falling in love makes you feel alive. An intimate encounter stimulates the same energy source that your subconscious mind uses to perform its magic. Keep that energy flowing.

If you already have a lover, renew the relationship and infuse it with a fresh dose of excitement. If you do not currently have a love interest, be available for one to come into your life. Open yourself emotionally to make room for any encounter that could lead to love. Be willing to explore whatever comes your way.

There is no better motivating force than love. For an extra push down the road to success, keep yourself receptive to the prospect of a loving relationship. Do not assume you are too old or too unattractive for a new or rekindled romance. You are not. Great things happen all the time, and people on the road to success expect them at every turn.

Look up.

Most people, as they grow older, droop. Gravity takes a heavy toll. Their faces sag. Their bodies sag. Their spirits sag. They end up hunched over, permanently staring at the floor.

That does not need to happen. Do not let it happen to you. You can be different. You can reject the depths and embrace the heights. You can look up.

At least once every day, make yourself gaze skyward. Actually bend your head back and look straight up. As you do so, think uplifting thoughts. Think of the direction up as the direction your life is headed. That's where you are going now. Whenever you notice yourself staring at the floor, raise your eyes and look upward. The physical act of looking up transmits a positive psychological message to your subconscious mind. Think up.

As much as possible, stand straight and hold your head high. Imagine you are immune to gravity. Picture your skin and your body naturally tending to lift, as if drawn upward by a magnetic force from the sky. Feel light and agile, quick on your feet. Stop focusing on burdens of life weighing you down; direct your attention to pleasures of life lifting you up. Down is wretched. Forget down. Up is the way to go.

Welcome change.

The past ended yesterday. The future starts today. Do not look back. Do not reminisce over bad times. When you focus on unpleasant past experiences, you reinforce their negative images. Who wants that? Put the past behind you and look to a bright and glorious tomorrow. Get excited about your future. You've got reason to get excited now.

When changes start happening in your life, welcome them. Do not try to resist or slow the tide of destiny. Sometimes when money starts flowing, it comes so fast and furious you get caught off guard. The natural re-action is to slow down, to bail out. Don't. Relax and let it happen. Welcome these new monetary events into your life. Celebrate the changes that come your way, for change is the transport to your new life.

Keep active.

Keep yourself in motion. Do not become physically lazy or mentally sluggish. Fashion a life-style that's lively and dynamic. Results are obtained by doing things.

Don't go too far with this idea, however. To achieve success, you do not need to work hard or push yourself to the limit of endurance. Do not exhaust yourself. All you need to do is keep some minimum degree of activity in your life.

This is not a bizarre concept. I merely suggest that you avoid falling into a rut in which you lay around all day doing nothing. Listlessness saps your strength and drains your creative energy. If you add a little activity to your life, everything improves.

AN ACTIVE BODY GROWS.
AN ACTIVE MIND EVOLVES.
AN ACTIVE LIFE PROSPERS.

Activity keeps your heart beating and your blood flowing. Activity keeps new ideas and new contacts circulating in your life. Activity keeps your subconscious mind pumped up and ready to go.

Leaving the light on...

For many years, I studied the behavior of successful men and women. I researched the lives of writers, artists, musicians, millionaires, politicians, industrialists and famous personalities. I discovered that, without exception, every one of the people I studied used the power of his or her subconscious mind, either knowingly or unknowingly. In every case, the person first had a vivid image of a goal firmly implanted in his or her mind. When you study the life of any person who achieved a measure of success—in any field of endeavor—you find that the person employed these same principles.

I do not mean to suggest that all successful people used affirmations. They didn't. But they did manage, somehow, to get an image of what they wanted into their subconscious mind. That much is certain. The affirmation technique I've shown you is the easiest way ever devised to do exactly the same thing, to get the images of your choice implanted into your subconscious mind.

Riches are shy. They are timid. They must be coyly attracted. And now you know a foolproof way to do just that. Wealth gravitates to those whose minds attract it, just as moths are drawn to those who leave the porch light on. When big money starts flowing into your life, it flows as effortlessly as water flows downhill. It has no other course of action open to it. Money must come your way. You better get ready for it.

Minimize
your
Repellant
force

"What goes around comes around."
Bob Dylan

7

The Law
of Repulsion

IN THE NEXT FOUR chapters, you will learn how to minimize the repellant force you generate toward money. You will discover the Law of Repulsion and learn a specific technique to reduce the force driving money from your life. If you apply this technique, you will experience abundance in everything you do.

Subtle forces influence every aspect of life. In our dynamic world, no force acts alone. Every force also implies its opposite force. And so it is with the forces acting on money.

In the previous section, you learned about the attractive force that draws money toward you. But this is not the only force affecting money. If it were, you'd constantly have all the money in the world, and no one could ever take one penny from you. Obviously, that is not the case.

Your attractive force is countered by your repellant force. At the same time your attractive force is pulling money toward you, your repellant force is pushing money away from you. This repellant force behaves in strict accordance with the Law of Repulsion.

The Law of Repulsion states: Addiction to any preconceived image of intelligence repels the manifestation of that image in reality. In other words, an addiction to a particular image tends to repel the materialization of anything that corresponds to that image.

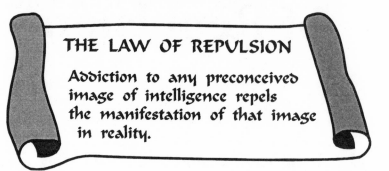

THE LAW OF REPULSION

Addiction to any preconceived image of intelligence repels the manifestation of that image in reality.

Let me ask you, "What is addiction?" You probably imagine a dirty, unshaven man in baggy clothes passed out in an alley with an empty bottle in his hand. He looks sickly, with greasy hair, transparent skin and track marks on his arm. He reeks of alcohol and body odor. As you lean forward to get a look, he squints an eye and belches a breath that could kill a moose. Quite a picture, huh? Although popular, this perception of addiction is outdated and inaccurate. Addiction, as it relates to money, is far more subtle—and far more common.

Inviting Anguish...

Webster's dictionary defines *addiction* as "enthusiastic devotion, strong inclination or frequent indulgence." For our purposes, think of addiction as "any compulsive need characterized by an emotion-backed demand."

The critical element is the emotion-backed demand. An addiction stands in sharp contrast to a desire, a preference or even a strong yearning. Unlike a desire, which expresses a longing, an addiction expresses a demand backed by a fierce, obsessive emotion. A person caught in addiction insists, with emotional fervor, that the demand be met. Whether or not an actual need for the object exists, an addiction carries with it a sense of urgent necessity. When an addiction is not satisfied, strong emotions that invite mental (and sometimes physical) anguish are activated.

An addiction is an internal ache that causes emotional upheaval if not appeased. Addiction imposes a mode of mental programming that activates uncomfortable emotions when the world does not conform to one's wishes. The fundamental characteristic of addiction, which sets it apart from mere desire, is that a person with addiction responds emotionally, feeling intense displeasure when a demand is not satisfied.

"If you have ever violated your values and ignored responsibilities to pursue an overpowering desire, then you understand the feeling of addiction."
Charlotte Davis Kasl

An addiction functions in one of two ways. It can be directed either at wanting to acquire something or at wanting to avoid something. In other words, an addiction can be in favor of a particular object or situation, or it can be opposed to an object or situation. However, as far as an addiction's destructive nature is concerned, the focal point of the addiction makes no difference. Either way, an addiction constitutes negative activity that is unproductive and ill-advised.

Lurking Behind Everything...

Our society inundates its population with media information. In the normal course of living, every individual receives thousands of subtle messages designed to create a feeling of dissatisfaction. Every day, people of all ages are bombarded with advertising whose message is that they are sexy only if they drive a luxury car, desirable only if they look like a movie star, happy only if they marry the person of their dreams and respectable only if they earn millions.

Addiction develops easily in this social environment. Everyone picks up an assortment of addictions, and no one even notices. People expect each other to have addictive tendencies. Addiction has become so prevalent that it passes for a normal state of affairs. Some people might display it more than others, but everyone, to some extent, carries within them the seeds of addiction.

"Everyone is an addict, one way or another."
Don Hamilton III

Addictive behavior is not exclusive to individuals, either. Entire groups—based on national or political affiliation—demonstrate addictive behavior. The waging of war stems from ideological disputes between groups of people clinging to their convictions. The long and painful saga of human history is easily understood in terms of misguided beliefs that result from unyielding addictive behavior.

Signs of addiction are everywhere. Our work, our play, our passions, all show unmistakable evidence of addiction. Behind almost everything we do, an addictive mindset is pulling the strings.

Is it any wonder, then, that so many people develop an addiction to money? Is it any surprise that most people don't even know they are addicted? Addiction is not always obvious, but it is always destructive.

Grinding up dreams...

Some addictions, such as to drugs or alcohol, lead to severe and obvious repercussions. Other addictions, such as to fame or money, do not cause obvious harm. These addictions seem to have a constructive or pleasurable component. Nonetheless, all addictions, no matter what their focus, have similar characteristics and lead to frustration and ineffectiveness in one form or another.

"The only difference between one addiction and another is the hook or experience which helps the addict manage life's highs and lows."
Susan Peabody

When you are addicted to something and cannot have it, you feel bad. If you get it and then lose it, you want it again and feel bad again. No matter what the object of addiction, unhappiness is inevitable.

If the addiction is severe, obsession fills your reality. You see your place in the world as a soldier, struggling to maintain a sense of balance, fighting to regain control of your destiny. Driven by insatiable craving, you live at the mercy of your addictive consciousness. Your desire lingers beneath everything you do. Everywhere you go, your addiction waits for you. Addiction steals your freedom, badgering you with visions of catastrophe. The panic is real, even if not outwardly visible. In the depth of your being, you feel alone, confused and disheartened.

Addiction is a state of powerlessness. More than two hundred different twelve-step organizations (such as Alcoholics Anonymous) are in operation today. They all deal with addiction in one form or another. Every one of them starts with a first step that declares: "We admitted we were powerless..." When you cross over the line from preference to addiction, you surrender your power, handing control of your life to your desires.

"Our addictions are our worst enemies. They enslave us with chains that are of our own making and yet that, paradoxically, are virtually beyond our control."
Gerald G. May

In extreme cases, addiction locks you into isolation. You shun friends, family and responsibilities. You see one thing only: the object of your addiction. This object demands all your attention. You arrange your life to accommodate your desperate search. Your first thought in the morning and last thought at night is a contemplation of how to fulfill your addiction. Nothing else is of any consequence to you.

You might manage to keep your outer appearance relatively intact, maintaining your job and relationships. Inside, however, your addiction is grinding up hopes and dreams as a meat grinder does beef. This is the calling card of addiction: a feeling of doom and frustration.

Even if you appear to derive some sense of pleasure as a result of your addiction, the pleasure is always shallow and short-lived. As soon as you satisfy the addiction, you worry about potential threats, real or imagined. You fret over supposed events that could take the pleasure from you. You compare today's pleasure with pleasures from the past, and the current pleasure comes up short. You plague yourself with anxiety, wondering whether you will be able to get the pleasure back if you lose it. Whatever fleeting enjoyment you cull from an addiction, it is a poor substitute for genuine happiness. When you are addicted, you worry. This is inescapable. You feel fear when you contemplate the prospect of nonfulfillment. You feel frustration when you encounter difficulty reaching fulfillment. You feel apprehension when you think of related outcomes. You feel jealousy when you picture someone stealing your source of fulfillment. You feel anger when events come between you and your fulfillment. You feel upset when you are undersupplied. You feel dread when you no longer see a steady supply. You feel panic when your supply dwindles. All these feelings lead to worry. You worry about everything. You even worry about being worried.

A severe addiction causes you to experience life in a distorted way, as if you were living in a series of theatrical events. You typically blow a minor problem out of proportion until it becomes a crisis. Your emotions rise to elated heights and fall to dismal depths. Tasks you perform take on historic proportions as you attempt to counter the spectacle of a dreary existence.

"Addicts live in excess and on the edge.
Because they do not complete things, they
have much unfinished business."
Patrick Carnes

Granted, these descriptions are extreme. Not every addiction exhibits these characteristics or produces disaster all the time. There are varying degrees of addiction, with symptoms becoming obvious only in severe cases. You can have a moderate addiction, show few signs, and appear normal to yourself and others. Nonetheless, every addiction, no matter how mild or unobtrusive, contains the same patterns. To whatever degree, addiction always fosters a negative state of mind that results in a measure of worry and unhappiness. The unfortunate fact is that none of this brutal agonizing and desperate activity brings you what you want.

Repelling things...

Everyone realizes that addiction fosters obsessive behavior and that it leads to unpleasant experiences for the addict. Everyone understands that addiction means frustration and hopelessness for people who suffer its grip. Few people realize, however, that addiction also repels the object of addiction. Not only does addiction breed discontent, it is an ineffective way of getting the object you desire in the first place.

Have you ever worried about something so much that your worst fear happened? Have you ever had such an intense addiction that, try as you may, you could never get the thing you wanted? The Law of Repulsion states that an addiction to an image repels its realization.

> *"Pushers are everywhere. But once you get hooked, where are they?"*
> Lenny Bruce

Life contains plenty of examples that show this law at work. The heroin addict struggles to find a fix. The bulimic is unable to buy sufficient food. The person addicted to sex cannot keep a steady partner. The person addicted to approval wrestles with self-doubt. The person addicted to money never has enough.

You probably prefer not to have an auto accident, right? I knew a man who did not just prefer it, he was addicted to the idea. He was forever worrying about an accident. He agonized over it every time he climbed into his car. Late last year, this man was involved in a terrible multi-car collision. The man was a safe driver, but his addiction to accident-free driving worked against him.

Most people assume that the more you "need" something, the more likely you are to get it. The opposite is true. The more you insist on something with an emotion-backed demand, the more you repel the thing from coming into your life. Conversely, when you reduce your addiction, you lessen your repellant force and increase the likelihood of getting what you want. This concept may strike you as paradoxical, but the logic is sound.

One note of caution: do not confuse an addiction with a visualization. The two are different. An addiction fosters a negative, destructive state of mind, which renders the addict incapable of effective action. By contrast, a healthy desire promotes a positive, uplifting state of mind, which allows for the conscious act of implanting an image. You can easily cultivate an image of something in your subconscious mind while, at the same time, remaining free of addiction.

Your subconscious mind does not respond favorably to addiction. Your mind abhors it, dreads it, hates it. Addiction causes you to feel unworthy. Your subconscious mind responds the only way it knows how, by shunning the object of addiction, by rejecting anything having to do with your obsessive desire—in short, by repelling it. When you become addicted to something, all the energy that normally gets devoted to manifesting the thing now gets devoted to repelling it.

Addiction leads to a cycle of pathologic behavior. The more the object of your addiction eludes you, the more desperate you become to secure it. The more desperate you become, the more frustrated you feel. The more frustrated you feel, the more obstacles you encounter trying to reach your goal. In other words, when you are addicted to something, the more difficult the thing is to obtain. Getting what you want appears to be the only way out, the only way to relieve your pain. This narrow-minded approach produces the opposite result of what you want, making the attainment of your goal more difficult.

"I'm afraid to get attached to anything anymore.
Every time I do, I lose it and can't get it back."
Doris Springer

Have you ever had the experience of being unable to remember a song title? You know the name of the song, you've heard it a thousand times, yet, no matter how hard you try, you cannot recall it. Then, when you finally give up and quit struggling to remember, the name pops into your mind. This illustrates the Law of Repulsion. As long as you are addicted to remembering, attached to the idea of knowing the name, your mind is turbulent and ineffective. As soon as you let go of your attachment to the outcome, the answer appears before you like a flash of lightning. This is the mechanism by which addiction repels things.

You may want to convince yourself that addiction is good for you, that it causes you to think intensely and constantly about your desire. Truth is, under the tyranny of addiction, you expend energy inefficiently. You waste resources and consciousness that could be used more effectively if you were not addicted.

When you are addicted to something, fate seems to push the object away from you by repelling helpful situations from your life and rendering your best-laid plans futile. Addiction has the power to counter whatever you do and keep you from achieving your goals.

Addiction is not evil or sinful, just unwise. It costs too much in lost effectiveness. Trying to reach your goals by clinging to them is always a lesson in futility.

Deflecting success...

People become addicted to many things. Sex, food, drugs, cars, sports, parties and television are frequent objects of addiction. People get addicted to power, prestige and popularity, too. A person can easily develop an addiction to a goal or an ambition, an idea or a prejudice, even a belief system or a position in life. Some people are addicted to the idea that they are not addicted, in which case they are addicted to their own denial! Every conceivable object, activity or situation serves as a potential target for addiction.

So, why not money? Thoughts of money occupy a large percentage of people's waking hours. Money plays a paramount role in the fortunes of life. The lure of riches is central to the functioning of society. Truth is, nearly everyone in our culture has some degree of addiction to money. Chances are, you do too.

Although you might have other addictions grinding away in your life, they are not at issue here. This discussion centers on your addiction to money. Don't think this topic has no relevance to you, because it does.

Regardless of who you are, you have some degree of monetary addiction. Maybe you don't exhibit visible symptoms. Maybe you don't fit addictive stereotypes.

Maybe you don't relate to the extreme descriptions of addiction presented a few pages back. No matter. You still carry an element of addiction to money. This is not an insult to you; it means you are a functioning member of contemporary society.

People with an addiction to money do not appear different from others. You cannot pick them out of a crowd. They are ordinary people who look and act like you or me. They are waiters, mechanics, architects, business-people, office workers, factory workers, whatever. They do not wear a sign announcing their addiction. Unlike acute alcoholics and drug addicts, they have not messed up their lives any more than the average person has. They do not hide in alleys and beg for spare change. The old stereotypes of an addict break down in the case of a typical man or woman addicted to money. The money addict is you, your cousin, your best friend.

Where does all this monetary addiction come from? Many places. Parents, teachers, and social conditioning all play a role. The addiction to money is so prevalent today that no one even recognizes it.

> *"Parents unknowingly pass their addictive perceptions of the world on to their children. Although children may switch their addictions, their addictive thinking remains the same."*
> Bryan Robinson

You do not need to be rich to be addicted to money. You can be flat broke and still bear the addiction. I have seen many low-income individuals nurse an uncontrollable addiction to the idea of wealth. Just as you do not need a large reserve of drugs to be a drug addict, you do not need a large bank balance to be a money addict.

If an addiction to money helped you attain a life of wealth and leisure, that would be one thing. In that case, you might argue that your affluence is worth the pain your addiction brings. But it does not. An addiction to money leads, instead, to a life of financial woe, a life of hard work and tight budgeting, a life of chronic debt and broken dreams. An addiction to money carries no redeeming value whatsoever.

When you live with an addiction to money, you live with failure. No matter what you try, you remain unable to touch the prize of an abundant life. Your addiction may be subtle and undetectable. It may not destroy your life in an obvious way. But deep inside, where your subconscious mind functions, the addiction is busily at work deflecting success from your life.

If you are trying to acquire wealth by maintaining an addiction to it, you will fail. Your addiction is a trap, like the trap that is used in India to catch monkeys. A trapper hollows out a coconut and cuts a hole in one end. The hole is barely large enough for the hand of a monkey to pass through. The trapper puts a tiny treat inside and attaches the coconut to a tree. Soon, a monkey comes along and reaches in to grab the food. When the monkey holds the treat in his hand, his fist can no longer pass through the hole. Rather than let go, the monkey remains trapped. Much like the monkey, most people would rather stay broke than release their addiction to money.

"There is nothing so habit-forming as money."
Don Marquis

Why should you face your addiction? Why not let your addictive behavior run rampant? What harm is done if you have a moderate degree of money addiction? These are thoughtful questions. Now, let me ask you something in return. Do you want to be successful? Do you want to eliminate financial worry from your life once and for all? If your answer is yes, you must face your addiction to money. It's as simple as that. Letting your addiction run rampant is exactly how you got into your fix in the first place. If you do nothing about the situation that confronts you, nothing will change.

An addiction is an emotional emergency, a competency crisis that devours you from the inside out. The time to reverse this grim prospect is now. You can do it. There's an easy way to fix things, and I'll show you how.

In the teachings of Buddhism, the Four Noble Truths are a central element of faith. Simply put, these truths say: (1) life contains suffering, (2) the cause of all suffering is addiction, (3) addiction can be overcome, and (4) there exist ways to do this. Take comfort in these truths. No matter how bleak things look right now, you are about to dig out of your hole. Freedom awaits you.

8

Upgrading
Your Addiction

DO YOU EVER WORRY about anything? Do you ever experience stress, anxiety or apprehension? Of course, you do. Everyone does at one time or another. Worry is a fact of life in today's society.

Worry is a state of mind based on fear, usually fear about an imagined event you think might happen or an impending outcome that would be unfavorable. Worry is a thief, a killer. It robs you of health, serenity and enjoyment of life. Slowly but steadily, it causes physical and emotional damage. A person laden with worry is a person that is miserable and unproductive.

Demolishing aspirations...

Worry is a reliable indicator of the presence of addiction. Whenever you feel the slightest hint of worry, a flag should go up telling you an addiction has been exposed. When you identify the source of your worry, you uncover the offending addiction.

According to surveys, the most common sources of worry in our society are, in order:

(1) Money
    insufficient funds, inability to buy material objects, high payments, financial security
(2) Health
    disease, aches and pains, medical emergencies and surgery, sickness of loved ones, effects of aging
(3) Family matters
    misbehaving children, marital problems, living arrangements, domestic abuse and violence
(4) Crime
    personal safety, home and auto security, gangs and urban problems
(5) Loneliness
    lack of companionship, shortage of friends, absence of love, scarcity of steady dates
(6) Job concerns
    dissatisfaction with work, problems with boss or fellow employees, job security
(7) Politics
    liberal and conservative causes, national issues, world affairs, prospects of war, ecological concerns
(8) Status
    social and peer pressures, conformity, anxiety concerning rumors
(9) Spirituality
    salvation vs. damnation, maintaining faith, living with reverence and devotion, converting others
(10) Life-styles
    indecision about life choices, procrastination, low self-esteem, identity crises

Notice that money tops the list. Money generates more worry than anything else in life. Money causes more emotional upheaval than matters of health, family, crime, loneliness, employment, politics, status, the world situation or even eternal damnation. Money may be the most popular object of addiction in the world today.

Is it any wonder that so many people face money problems? Nine out of ten people who seek professional counseling admit they worry about money. Some can't pay bills. Some can't keep a job. Some can't even earn enough to buy groceries. Without the money to live as they want, they feel inadequate and ashamed. They feel they've disappointed those who believed in them. An addiction to money, they have—money, itself, they don't.

Can you be counted among this group? If you ever worry about anything relevant to your financial situation, then you possess some degree of addiction to money. Don't think you are exempt from this subject. If you worry about money, or ever have, this discussion is aimed squarely at you.

"A billion dollars in the bank, without the experience of carefreeness and charity, is a state of poverty."
Deepak Chopra

Wake up. Your addiction is killing you. Quietly, but undeniably, it is demolishing your aspirations and gutting your chances for success. You need to deal with your addiction to money sooner rather than later.

Aligning with freedom...

So, you want to get rid of your addiction. You want to kill it, destroy it, annihilate it once and for all. Okay, I understand the sentiment, but that is not the way to deal with addiction. You cannot eliminate an addiction the way you would crush a bug under your foot. There is another way, a better way, the only way. What you need to do to free yourself from addiction is this:

YOU MUST UPGRADE YOUR ADDICTION TO A PREFERENCE.

Understand this concept, because it is important. The way to disable an addiction, to render it ineffective, is not to suppress it or destroy it. What you must do is upgrade it to a preference. This is not a play on words. Upgrading an addiction to a preference constitutes a fundamental transformation regarding the way you approach desire.

To understand this process, you must understand the difference between an addiction and a preference. Your emotional outlook determines whether you have an addiction or a preference. With an addiction, you feel worry. When you focus on the object of your addiction, you experience emotional tension, which stems from a sense of fear or dread. You have an emotion-backed demand, which creates concern about perceived threats and gives you a sense of dissatisfaction. You worry that you won't get what you want, won't get enough of it or won't be able to hang onto it if you do get it. With an addiction, even when it's satisfied, you immediately worry about keeping what you have, which perpetuates the addiction.

With a preference, you feel peace. When you contemplate the object in question, you do not experience mental responses that stem from fear, jealousy or apprehension. Instead, you feel clarity and composure.

You simply notice the feelings and situations that exist. With a preference, you are free to act from a position of confidence and keen thinking.

Suppose you are planning a long bike ride in the country on Saturday. The day comes. You load your bike with the essentials for your trip. You prepare a wonderful lunch to eat along the way. You feel great and are raring to go. And then it rains. Rain beats down so hard you cannot see ten feet in front of you. With an attitude of addiction, you become enraged. Your whole day is shot. You wonder why this sort of thing always happens to you. Anger and frustration rage inside your body. The remainder of your day is spent coping with this unpleasant turn of events.

With an attitude of preference, you simply notice that rain is falling and that you will be unable to fulfill your desire. You gather your wits, unpack your bike and go inside. You might call a friend, read a book or play on the computer. Later, you partake of a delicious lunch at your kitchen table. You enjoy the rest of the day to its fullest, taking in whatever life has to offer. The day turns out to be wonderful. When you operate from the vantage point of a preference, there is no way anything can detract from your enjoyment of the moment.

> *"Life is not just a matter of holding good cards,*
> *but sometimes of playing a poor hand well."*
> Robert Louis Stevenson

When an addiction is not satisfied, you are unhappy. When a preference is not satisfied, you are indifferent—after all, it is only a preference. When you have an addiction, you feel trapped, caged by menacing thoughts. When you have a preference, you feel free, released into a world of infinite possibility. An addiction always leads to unhappiness, one way or another. A preference never does.

ADDICTION ALIGNS WITH BONDAGE. PREFERENCE ALIGNS WITH FREEDOM.

When you have a desire, there are two possible outcomes: either your desire is met, or it is not. With an addiction, if your desire is not met, you are miserable. If your desire is met, you are still miserable. You may feel some momentary relief, but the relief does not last. You soon resume your life of struggle as you attempt to hang on to your brief moment of pleasure.

With a preference, if your desire is not met, you feel okay. You do not view your desire from the standpoint of desperation. When your desire is met, however, you feel elation. With a preference, you are free to experience the exhilaration of the moment in all its splendor. You do not need to immediately guard against supposed threats to your pleasure. Since you do not depend on an external situation for your happiness, you are free to savor the texture and magnificence of events as they occur in your life. Upgrading an addiction to a preference sets you free to fully experience whatever is happening, even if you prefer something different.

Reprogramming the mind...

The act of upgrading an addiction to a preference is an internal process. When you perform this upgrade, you reprogram the part of your mind that normally calls for a reaction of frustration, restlessness and unhappiness when your desire is not realized. You reprogram your unsettled mind so that it remains content regardless of the prognosis for getting what you want. The actual change, the mental shift that occurs when an addiction transforms into a preference, is a change of programming within your mind. External circumstances do not constitute your addiction. Only your internal, emotional programming determines the nature of your addiction. This programming is what you must target for change. This you can do. Making the shift from addiction to preference is easy once you know how.

> *"Nothing has changed but my attitude.*
> *Everything has changed."*
> Anthony DeMello

Understand that your life-style and living patterns need not change when this shift occurs. If you so choose, you can go on doing the things you've always done in the ways you've always done them. Upgrading an addiction to a preference is a process that occurs internally, affecting the emotional programming contained within your mind. This change need not have any bearing on your behavior. You can continue to do whatever you prefer to do—but without the undercurrent of addiction. When you remove addiction from the equation, your actions are characterized by insight and wisdom.

Until now, you may have been struggling to manipulate the outside world in order to satisfy your addictions. From now on, you'll approach life in a new way. You will now attack problems at their source, healing addictive mental programming lodged in your mind. You will then be able to make informed choices based on rational preference as opposed to stumbling through life led by neurotic addiction. This shift in perspective does not mean you turn your back on your desires; it means you release your obsessive way of relating to them. Upgrading an addiction to a preference reveals a world of fresh possibilities.

An addiction is always unnecessary. You can do the same things and have the same experiences without addiction dragging you down. You can embrace every wonderful circumstance life has to offer without your mind being burdened by addiction. An addiction does not function more effectively or let you have more fun than a preference does. In fact, you accomplish more and enjoy life more when you do not have addiction cluttering your mind.

Once an addiction changes to a preference, things you desire come to you more quickly and with less effort than before. And you no longer need to exhaust yourself with worry. The price you pay for maintaining and protecting an addiction is immense. Converting an addiction to a preference is the best way to cut your losses. It is the smart thing to do.

Do not think of upgrading an addiction as suppression. When you suppress a desire, you send your feelings down, hiding them, burying them. When you upgrade an addiction, you send your feelings up, elevating them to the plateau of a clear-minded preference. The shift from addiction to preference occurs not by inhibiting your feelings or by limiting your thinking, but by intentionally reprogramming your mind.

When you suppress something, you refuse to look at the thing because you fear your feelings about it. Suppression is an ineffective way to interact with the world around you. By contrast, the process of upgrading an addiction to a preference promotes a willingness to see what lies before you. You consciously take hold of your feelings and convert your addiction to the lofty realm of a preference. You do not suppress your vital energy; you employ your energy constructively to loosen the chains of addiction. The more conscious you become, the freer you become.

Performing the shift...

Are you sick and tired of money going out instead of coming in? Are you fed up with your monetary addiction repelling money from you? Then you need to upgrade your addiction to a preference. I urge you to perform this upgrade now.

Some people feel hesitant to modify their monetary addiction, fearful that, when they no longer have their addiction, they might lose their motivation to succeed. Do not let that idea concern you. Experience shows that once a person upgrades his or her monetary addiction, motivation increases.

You can still do whatever you want to do after your addiction is upgraded. The only difference is that you will no longer be addicted to any particular outcome as a result of your actions. After you upgrade your addiction to a preference, you are still free to actively seek money with your life's activities. After all, you still *prefer* to have money, right? The only change is that, since you are no longer repelling money from your life, whatever you do to make money works more effectively than it did when you were addicted. The upgrade from an addiction to a preference affects only your internal, emotional programming and nothing more. You lose nothing. You gain everything.

One day, I had a long talk with a woman who desperately wanted to get pregnant and had not been able to do so. She told me that having a baby was her strongest desire in life. I asked her if she felt she might be "addicted" to the idea of getting pregnant. She admitted she was. I suggested that she mentally reprogram her mind to shift that addiction to a preference.

At first, the woman was horrified. She was concerned that if she merely "preferred" to get pregnant, she would lack the motivation necessary to continue trying. She and her husband were about to embark on a series of medical procedures, and she felt she would need a great deal of determination to proceed. I assured her that if she shifted her attitude to a preference, her motivation would not suffer. I told her that she would actually become *more* effective at whatever she did.

That day a subtle change occurred in this woman. She lightened up. She still preferred to be pregnant, but the desperation—the addiction—was gone. Acting on her preference, she went ahead with her plans to get medical help. Her clarity of thought allowed her to focus her motivation on what needed to be done. She was able to work with her doctor calmly and rationally. Less than one year later, she gave birth to healthy baby girl.

> *"What you do may not seem important, but*
> *it is very important that you do it."*
> Mahatma Gandhi

After your consciousness shifts from an addiction to a preference, you experience far less pressure surrounding everything you do. You feel emotionally okay with whatever happens. Don't worry, you do not give up anything worthwhile in performing this shift. Adjusting your internal programming is all you do when you upgrade an addiction to a preference. You can still act as you always have, if that's what you prefer.

At first glance, the idea of converting your monetary addiction to a preference in order to lure money might seem paradoxical. You are decreasing an addiction as a way to increase money. Strange as the idea may sound, that is precisely how the Law of Repulsion works. When you become able to do without money—at a gut level, all joking aside—then, surprisingly, money flows your way in greater abundance than you thought possible. When you release yourself from the addiction to money, money comes your way. As soon as you do not absolutely need it, you will have it. That is how things work.

Here's a little secret: the way to prosperity and happiness is through acceptance. And just think, all these years you may have been going about things in exactly the wrong way! Now, I'll show you the right way.

*"When your wants are emptied, all great
rewards come to you."*
Lao Tzu

To upgrade an addiction to a preference, you must be sincere. You cannot simply say, "Okay, all my addictions are now preferences." That won't do. There is no deceit in this. You must have the proper automatic, emotional responses programmed in your mind. Your conversion must be heartfelt and penetrating.

If you have the ability to say, "Presto," and instantly convert your addiction to a preference by sheer force of will, great; I'm glad for you. I doubt, however, you can do this. To achieve the depth of mental programming required for this conversion, you need a gentle touch.

In the last section, when I told you to implant the images of your choice into your subconscious mind, I did not simply turn you loose to do it in whatever fashion you could figure out for yourself. No, I gave you specific instructions to accomplish the task, namely, affirmations. Likewise, in this section, I give you specific instructions to convert your money addiction to a money preference. Even if you do not understand exactly what new mental attitude you're trying to achieve or what this new consciousness feels like, don't worry. Follow my instructions, and you cannot fail to make the conversion. Do as I say, and you will definitely upgrade your monetary addiction to a preference.

The method I am about to describe will get this whole conversion process happening for you. Before long, you will realize that you are no longer addicted to money. You will notice that all worry and anxiety once associated with your financial situation have evaporated. By doing this technique, you will minimize the force that has been repelling money from your life—and money will shower down upon you.

9

Glad-Giving

THE METHOD DESCRIBED IN this chapter upgrades your monetary addiction to a preference. The method is called "glad-giving." It is a specific discipline that targets your addiction to money.

Glad-giving is a system of giving in which you donate a set percentage of your income to others. You must give the money freely without demands or conditions, and you must have no expectation of repayment.

At first glance, this method may strike you as peculiar. Giving away some of your money may seem like a ridiculous way to solve your money problems, since you might not have even enough money for yourself right now. Maybe you think no sane person would give away money. I understand your feelings.

If this idea sounds weird to you, take comfort in the fact that it sounds weird to everyone at first. If glad-giving sounds unattractive, don't be disillusioned. You will see that it is the answer you've been looking for.

Please, do not pass judgment yet. Let me tell you more. I want you to know exactly what glad-giving is and what it will do for you.

Generating more wealth...

Nothing in life is static. Everything flows in a constant state of exchange. And so it is with money. In order to receive, you must also give. The notion of an energy exchange is a fundamental concept relevant to the acquisition of wealth.

For you to receive money, money must circulate. If you hinder the movement of money out of your life, you block the flow. And if you block the flow, you halt the circulation of money back into your life, as well. Your money is like your blood: it must flow or the whole system comes to a stop. Hoarding money results in stagnation. In order to keep money coming into your life, you need to keep money circulating.

If the prospect of giving away money scares you, don't let it. There is plenty more money available for you. If the idea of donating money sounds repugnant, relax. There is no shortage of money in the world. Whatever money you give away, you will get back, and then some. Do not be afraid to part with money. In the process of letting go of cash, you are letting go of addiction. Don't worry, the money will return. As long as money is circulating, it will come your way again.

"Money is always there, only the pockets change."
Gertrude Stein

An apple seed carries within it the promise of an apple tree. But the seed must not be saved or locked in a vault.

To fulfill its promise, the seed must be given to the earth. Only through the act of giving does the promise of an apple tree burst into manifestation. In a similar way, when you give money to others, you awaken the powers that manifest money in your own life.

The practice of giving is based on age-old wisdom. In ancient times, donations were meant to acknowledge God's ownership of the soil and its fruits. Donations were distributed to the widowed, the fatherless and those without land to produce crops for themselves. The Hebrews considered a discipline of giving to be a practice of virtue. Jesus Christ also taught its benefits.

The concept of sharing whatever good you receive derives from natural law. Some teachings refer to this as the Law of Reciprocation. This law says that every individual gets out of life what he or she is willing to give. Energy returns to you in proportion to that which you put out; only the form of the energy changes. When this law is ignored, you experience hardship. When this law is observed, you experience an increase in the flow of supply into your life.

When you practice glad-giving, you reduce your addiction to money. Once that happens, your repellant force decreases and your flow of money increases. The benefits of glad-giving extend to every area of life. People who apply this method do not worry about money, yet they grow in wealth. Amazing as this fact sounds, it is undeniably true.

"Give and it shall be given unto you. Good measure, pressed down and running over shall be given unto your bosom. For with the same measure that you give, it shall be measured unto you again."
Luke 6:38

Do not mistake glad-giving for tithing. Tithing is a religious term that describes the requirement of donating a tenth of your income to the church. For centuries, tithing has been enforced in European church-states as an additional form of tax. Tithing carries dubious connotations, even today. The word reminds many people of the Sunday collection basket. By comparison, glad-giving focuses on upgrading your monetary addiction and increasing the flow of money into your life. Due to these fundamental differences, I prefer to disassociate the term glad-giving from the term tithing.

Simply put, glad-giving is the practice of giving away a set percentage of your income for the purpose of upgrading your monetary addiction to a preference. This upgrade reduces the force repelling money from your life, making money easier to obtain.

Maybe this concept strikes you as contradictory. After all, how could giving away money result in having more money? Well, it does. Regardless of how glad-giving works, it ends up generating more income than does hoarding your money. The simple truth is that glad-giving results in a life of abundance.

> *"The universe operates through dynamic exchange. In our willingness to give that which we seek, we keep the abundance of the universe circulating in our lives."*
> Deepak Chopra

Let me make clear that glad-giving is not indiscriminate giving. It is a discipline with rules to follow. To make it work, you must know what you are doing.

In adopting a practice of glad-giving, you need to look at three areas of consideration: how much to give, where to give and when to give. Each of these three topics is discussed in detail in the following pages.

Feeling it slightly...

The first question to consider is how much money to give. The amount is based on a percentage of your income. Designating a set number of dollars is inadvisable because a constant sum is not fair to everyone. A rich person could donate a particular amount without feeling a pinch, while a poor person would be unable to afford that same amount. Even within your lifetime, you could afford a certain amount at one time and not at another time. Since you do not earn the same income throughout life, donating a constant sum is impractical. A percentage equalizes this. A set percentage is fair to everyone and stays constant. The more you earn, the more you give, although the percentage remains unchanged.

The best figure falls within the range of 1 to 5 percent of your income. In other words, do not go below 1 percent or above 5 percent.

Many years ago, when I first started my personal program of glad-giving, I used a guideline of 10 percent. When I began instructing others in glad-giving, this was the percentage I suggested they try. That was a long time ago. In the years since, I have learned that this percentage is not optimal for the purpose of minimizing one's repellant force. Truth is, there is nothing special about 10 percent. For the purpose of generating a flow of money, 10 percent is higher than need be. A figure of 1 to 5 percent is plenty.

I arrived at these figures not through guesswork, but through a large body of research. For years, I conducted in-depth interviews that documented varying degrees of success. The findings show that the effectiveness of this method declines when the applied percentage drops below 1 percent or rises above 5 percent. That's not to say that another percentage, such as 10 percent, does not work at all. It does. But for most people, best results occur in the range of 1 to 5 percent.

Specifically, here's what I recommend you do. Start by designating 1 percent of your income for glad-giving. See how that feels. If you feel comfortable with that amount and you see good results, stay with it. If, on occasion, you feel compelled to give a little more, do so. If, overall, you feel the inclination to raise the percentage, and you can afford to do it, then go ahead and increase the figure. Over time, adjust the percentage to whatever value feels comfortable for you, up to a figure of 5 percent. Remember, for optimal results, do not go above 5 percent or below 1 percent.

In most cases, giving 1 percent is just fine; you need not feel any nagging that you should give more than that. However, remarkable as it sounds, many individuals choose to give a higher percentage. People have told me that, although they feel great at 1 percent, they feel three times better at 3 percent. A man once told me that he noticed his blood pressure reading was inversely proportional to his glad-giving percentage—the more he gave the lower his systolic figure.

I realize you are not practicing glad-giving to feel good. Your motivation, plain and simple, is to create a flow of money into your life. However, feeling good is a nice side effect when it happens. To find your best percentage, a reasonable rule of thumb is that you should not be hurt by the amount you give, but you should feel it slightly.

Maybe you're wondering: why not give more than 5 percent? Isn't it logical that the more you give, the better? Actually, no. Experience shows that when the percentage approaches 10 percent, hardship becomes too great. And when your level of discomfort rises, you feel dislike for your program of glad-giving. I have known people who start out full of enthusiasm, determined to give 10 percent or more. Within a few months, they have abandoned the whole idea, convinced it doesn't work.

This process should not be a struggle. Glad-giving is not intended as a backbreaking effort, a trying and demanding excursion into agony. Glad-giving should be inviting and easily doable. Furthermore, glad-giving's effectiveness at upgrading addiction does not improve at figures above 5 percent. Apparently, the mere act of committing to a program of giving does the trick. In terms of results, the actual percentage seems largely irrelevant—provided it does not drop below 1 percent or climb above 5 percent.

Again, do not equate glad-giving with tithing. Tithing insists on 10 percent. This figure originated in biblical times. Needless to say, social conditions are vastly different now. Compared to our ancestors, we live in a different world with different life-styles. In the information age, everyone knows about percentage brackets. We find them on tax forms, bank statements and stock reports. Even the waiter at the restaurant commands 15 percent these days.

So, why, if 10 percent was the favored figure two thousand years ago, does 1 to 5 percent work best now? I can only guess. The answer appears to be that a figure of 1 to 5 percent today translates into approximately the same power of giving as 10 percent did in ancient times.

Money today is highly scrutinized; every penny is watched. Apparently, a figure of 10 percent, which may have been fine for people of millennia past, is too intense for people of modern times.

By recommending 1 to 5 percent, I do not mean to contradict religious tradition or the teachings of any particular church. If you tithe for religious reasons, feel free to give 10 percent. Your giving will still produce favorable results. I am merely stating that, for the purpose of upgrading addiction, giving 1 to 5 percent is sufficient.

Research clearly shows that this range is preferable for most people. I use these percentages for my own glad-giving, and results have been phenomenal. Every person I know who gives between 1 and 5 percent gets results. This range is comfortable: it's not so small that it is ineffective, and it's not so large that it causes hardship.

Aiming energy...

At some point, you must decide who is to receive your monetary gifts. Although where you give your money is entirely up to you, a few guidelines can help produce the best results.

The first question is whether to give your money to individuals or to organizations—or to a combination of both. This is a question you must answer for yourself. There are advantages and concerns with each of these two types of donations.

Do not feel that giving to organizations is better, that unless you donate to some official cause, your efforts are less effective. Such is not the case. Feel free to base any or all of your glad-giving on donations to individuals. Over the years, I have given enormous sums of money to people I know.

When you give money to an individual, your glad-giving takes on a personal dimension. Typically, you know the person, or at least have some personal contact with him or her. You can give money to friends, relatives or complete strangers.

Although direct contact can be rewarding, there is a consideration with this approach, something you need to watch for. Remember, for glad-giving to be effective, the money must be given freely, without strings attached. That is not always easy to do when dealing with friends and associates. They usually want to repay you. This issue does not come up when donating to organizations; they regularly accept donations, and the concept of repayment does not arise. When you give to people you know, however, they often interpret the money as a loan. Even if you insist that the money is not to be repaid, people often feel indebted, obliged to pay you back anyhow. And when they do not pay you back, they end up feeling guilty. For this reason, I advise caution.

If you find someone who can accept your money as freely as you give it, great. (Giving to people you know can be a beautiful way to practice glad-giving.) If not, I suggest you confine your gifts to organizations. You decide how much of your glad-giving should go to people with whom you are in personal contact and how much should go to organizations.

If you decide to donate to organizations, pick ones you think are worthwhile. A group you select should be engaged in something you feel good about, exerting what you consider to be a positive influence on society. Ideally, any organization to which you contribute money should share the same ideological beliefs you do. This not only makes you feel better, but yields better results. When you give money, you are aiming your energy at a target. That target should be one you want to hit. Giving to an organization whose views run contrary to yours does not produce the same quality of experience as giving to a group whose convictions you support.

With some organizations, you are given the option of joining and receiving membership privileges. For example, a particular group may charge fifty dollars for a one-year membership. In return you receive a subscription to their newsletter. Do not think that because an organization sends you something, your gift is somehow undermined. Your fifty dollars is still a donation. As long as you donate of your own free will, you can count your donation as glad-giving. In fact, becoming a member of numerous organizations is an excellent way to practice glad-giving.

If you want, you can select one particular organization and always donate your money there. Or, you can pick a small number of organizations (maybe five or so) and earmark your glad-giving for those few. Or, you can spread your donations over any number of different organizations (perhaps dozens or more) and give small amounts to each one. As far as effectiveness is concerned, any of these approaches, or any combination of them, is fine. No one approach is perfect for everyone. You need to evaluate what feels right for you.

It is easy to discover worthwhile groups to which you want to contribute. Keep your eyes and ears open. Once you become attuned to donating money, you are always hearing about some organization doing something you support. When watching television, you may see a commercial that shows the wide-eyed face of a hungry child. If the message touches your heart, jot down the number and give them a call. When reading the newspaper, you may see an ad for a political campaign. If you'd like to join the effort, rip out the ad and send some money. When talking with friends, you may hear someone mention a charity he supports. If you identify with the cause, ask him for the address and mail an offering.

If you do not have sufficient information on a group to determine whether you want to donate, write to them and ask for literature. Most organizations are more than willing to send promotional material showing what they do. Seeing printed information before sending money is a smart policy.

There is no shortage of worthwhile organizations to which you can donate money. As of 1996, in the United States alone, there exist more than twenty thousand different national organizations pursuing their causes and vying for your support. They come in all varieties. They can be categorized as trade, health, sports, hobby, ethnic, social, business, veterans, cultural, fraternal, religious, scientific, vocational and so on. More than four thousand organizations are devoted to business, over two thousand to cultural issues, and over two thousand to medical concerns. Thousands more focus on recreation and having fun. If you are looking to contribute to an organization, plenty exist to take your money.

Listing places...

Appendix B (pg. 249) contains a short list of national organizations. The list is intended as a possible reference when you select groups for donations. You can pick and choose from this list if you are so inclined.

The list can be a useful resource to kick off your program of glad-giving. The organizations are categorized according to their area of interest, with each entry showing the organization's name, address, phone number, and year of inception. Also included is a brief statement summarizing who they are.

I tried to make the list as balanced as possible, providing something for everyone. I took care to insure that both liberal and conservative viewpoints were represented. To my knowledge, this is the only list ever compiled to specifically catalogue a wide variety of places worthy of receiving donations.

Keep in mind that the list is not all-inclusive; only a fraction of worthwhile organizations are listed. When you select places for glad-giving, be sure to consider local groups. Almost every city has community clinics, crisis hot-lines, animal rescue leagues, shelters for battered women, support groups for the handicapped, and soup kitchens for the homeless. Many people prefer to donate to these groups since the contact is often more personal. Finding organizations is easy and fun. If you have your own ideas about where to give money, then you never need to look at the list in Appendix B.

Setting a timetable...

The next consideration is *when* to make your donations. This one is easy. The general rule is: give when you get.

Figure out a schedule based on the frequency with which you receive income. If you get paid weekly, give weekly; if you get paid monthly, give monthly. Set your timetable and stick to it.

Do your glad-giving as soon as you get paid. Let's say you have a new job and you just received your first paycheck. Make your donation immediately—yes, even after your first check. Do not put it off. And continue to give promptly with every check you receive. If you are self-employed and your timetable is flexible, then base your glad-giving on a reasonable and comfortable schedule that aligns with your rate of income. If you are unemployed and receive money irregularly, follow the rule and give immediately whenever you obtain money.

You might think that, in your case, you would find it more convenient to practice glad-giving on a different schedule than one based on when you receive money. For example, you get paid weekly but would prefer to give monthly. I advise against this practice. Do not put your glad-giving on a different schedule than your pay. Doing so causes you, sooner or later, to delay or miss payments. I have seen many well-intentioned people struggle as a result of a misaligned schedule. A timetable coordinated with your pay is decidedly more effective. There is a certain quality of experience that occurs when you consistently *give when you get*.

Calculating money...

The recommendation to give when you get is good advice. But there's more. The corollary to that rule is: give *only* when you get. If you give only when you get, you will never give too much or too little—or too soon.

The concept is simple: give in accordance with whatever money you actually "see." In other words, consider only money that actually passes through your hands as money that is subject to glad-giving. If someone promises you money in thirty days, wait until you get the money before you give a percentage away. When the money is in your hands, then, and not before, proceed with your glad-giving.

Always base your glad-giving on your take-home pay. Do not worry about money you've earned that has been deducted from your paycheck. If, at the end of the year, you get a tax refund, then give at that time. Do not give when you figure out your taxes and know the amount the refund will be; wait until you get the refund check in your hands before you give. If you always conduct your glad-giving this way, based on money you actually see, you will never give any more or any less than you should, and everything will check out in the end.

Calculating money for glad-giving is easy. Suppose your income is $5,000 per month. Your take-home pay, after taxes and deductions, is $4,000 per month. In that case, use $4,000 as the base from which to calculate your glad-giving. If you select a figure of 1 percent for glad-giving, you would donate exactly $40 of your income each month. That's all. The $40 figure is arrived at by multiplying 1 percent (or .01) by $4000. If you use a figure of 3 percent for glad-giving, you would donate 3 percent of $4000 (.03 × $4000), which is $120. If you decide to give 5 percent, you would multiply .05 by $4000, yielding a figure of $200 each month for glad-giving.

Imagine you win the lottery for $5,000,000. The state pays you, not in one lump sum, but in increments of $20,000 each month for the next 25 years. Assuming a figure of 1 percent for glad-giving, you would give away $200 (.01 × $20,000) per month. This is the obvious way to handle this situation. The alternative is to suddenly be obligated for 1 percent of the entire $5,000,000 at the moment you win the lottery. You would need to come up with a grand total of $50,000 on the spot. Clearly, this approach is absurd. Remember the rule: give only when you get.

When figuring your income tax, feel free to claim your donations as tax-deductible contributions. Doing so does not detract from the effectiveness of glad-giving. Claiming donations saves you money on taxes, and there's no reason to feel guilty about that. You may as well get all the tax breaks you are due. In general, I say go ahead and take whatever money you can get, as long as you are honestly entitled to it. Do whatever you can to earn money and manage it effectively. Do not become careless or indiscriminate with money. Glad-giving is not sloppy. Glad-giving is a strict discipline requiring careful money management.

Any money you acquire, no matter how you get it, should be considered income at that precise moment. Do not deny any funds you receive. Acknowledge every bit of money that comes your way and earmark a percentage of it for glad-giving.

Glad-giving is not an on-again, off-again proposition. Do your glad-giving consistently. Don't start, then stop, then start again. You must make your donations regularly or results never hit full force. Consistency is key. Decide to adopt glad-giving as a way of life, and then do it. Donate at least 1 percent of every paycheck you get. Don't miss one paycheck out of five and hope nobody notices. Commit yourself to this method without cutting corners. You'll be glad you did.

Jumping the hurdle...

The trickiest part of glad-giving is getting started. You need willpower and discipline to actually sit down, write out that first check and mail it away. You may find your first few donations difficult to make, especially since no one is standing over you forcing you to make them.

You really don't *need* to do this program. You could just as easily forget this whole thing, and no one would know the difference—except you.

> "*A pupil from whom nothing is ever demanded never does all he can.*"
>
> John Stuart Mill

Early in this book, I asked you something. I want to ask it again now. Do you really want financial security? Be honest. The question is not as trivial as it appears. Some people actually "like" to be miserable. They like the constant barrage of money problems and financial hassles. They may claim they want to be free of money worries, but when it comes to actually *doing* something about the situation, they balk. So, you must ask yourself this question and get a truthful answer.

Do you really want total financial security? Does the prospect of financial freedom set your heart aflutter? Do you long for it? Can you taste it? Now, the most crucial question of all: Do you want it badly enough to actually do something about it? Do you want it badly enough to at least give this method a try? If your answer is no, that's okay. I appreciate your honesty. If your answer is yes, great! Then you can have it. I repeat: *you can have it!* Total financial security is yours if you want it! Glad-giving is a significant step in that direction.

I will give you a pointer on getting started. Here is something you can do to ease your initial foray into the world of glad-giving. You can change your way of looking at your income. Do not think of all your take-home pay as "yours." Until now, you have probably considered your income to be the full amount you get paid. Change that way of thinking. Mentally deduct the amount of glad-giving before considering your income.

Let's assume you decide to devote 3 percent of your income to glad-giving. If your take-home pay is $4,000 per month, consider instead that your pay is only $3,880 per month. Deduct 3 percent of $4,000 (which is $120) from $4,000. Think only in terms of $3,880 per month. Tell your friends you make $3,880. When budgeting, planning a vacation, saving for college or whatever, think in terms of $3,880 spendable income per month. Do not consider, in any thinking, that $4,000 exists or ever did exist. The $4,000 is not yours. If someone asks you how much you earn, say $3,880 a month. Get used to the new figure. This shift in thinking makes getting started easier.

Anything you can do to nudge yourself to begin, do it. Getting started takes discipline. Do not be surprised if you try to talk yourself out of it. Glad-giving is not difficult, but the task of putting this plan into action looks enormous at first. The idea of giving away a portion of your hard-earned cash seems dreadful. Be prepared to jump this hurdle.

"You must do the thing you think you cannot do."
Eleanor Roosevelt

Ultimately, your program of glad-giving is your responsibility. You decide how much to give, where to give and when to give. You are the one in charge here. My recommendations are based on a knowledge of what works and what other people have found effective. But the decision to act—and how to act—is yours alone. In the final analysis, you are in charge of what you do, just as you are in charge of what happens in your life.

Relieving financial problems...

Many years ago, I was flat broke. I had no money whatsoever to my name. I lived in a desperate state, drifting from job to job. I never accumulated enough cash to do anything worthwhile.

At one point, I was staying in a roach-infested hotel in Berkeley, California and living off charity from a few friends. I had just borrowed $100, purchased an old, beat-up Studebaker and was attempting to drive to my new job, selling magazines. As I headed down the road, the car made a horrendous racket and belched black smoke. Then the thing blew up. There I stood by the side of the road, broke, hungry and responsible for a useless hunk of metal sitting in everyone's way. I walked to work and was promptly fired. That was a low point.

Was it hard for me to start glad-giving at that time? You bet it was. But I did it anyway. I didn't expect it to work, either. But it did. Today, I have no more monetary worries. As I write this, I sit at my desk in a wonderful mountain home nestled deep in the trees. Everything I need, I have. I couldn't be happier with how my life has unfolded.

How did I go from a state of destitution to where I am today? I'll tell you this: it was *not* a result of hard work and backbreaking drudgery. Glad-giving reduced my addiction to money, which allowed money to flow into my life. Needless to say, I wholeheartedly believe in the effectiveness of glad-giving. I still give regularly, and I intend to go on giving for as long as I live.

A man and his wife were in a frantic situation when they heard about glad-giving. He was unemployed, and she had just given birth to their third child. They had depleted their savings and were expecting to be homeless at the end of the month. The cost of diapers and baby formula added to their difficulties. They started glad-giving. In fact, I gave them the twenty-dollar bill from which they made their first fifty-cent donation. From that day on, their financial situation improved. Eventually, he got a job with a large company and worked his way up to department head. Not only did they never become homeless, but they moved into a beautiful home in the country. Today, they have no more financial worries, and all their needs are promptly and easily met.

I know a young man, just twenty-two years old, who used this method several times for particular goals. He attributes his new sports car to a specific instance of glad-giving. "I've heard at least a thousand testimonies of people who give," Wayne said to me recently, "and I haven't heard a bad account yet. I don't know of a single person who ever gave who did not get back more than they gave as a result."

A middle-aged woman started glad-giving about two years ago. At that time, she was deeply in debt and had family problems involving domestic violence. Since then, her wealth has skyrocketed and her family troubles have been resolved. Today, her standard of living easily ranks among the top percentage of Americans. What is interesting about her case is that she has not changed jobs or taken any other specific steps that would account for the improvement in her life. A few investments paid off, a few personal matters worked out favorably, and that's all. Other than that, nothing changed, except for the fact that she started glad-giving. Ask her about glad-giving, and she'll talk your ear off.

I've instructed many thousands of people on glad-giving, and there are many success stories I could tell.

But understand this: for every individual, the hardest part is starting. In times of hardship, giving away a percentage of your income seems foolish. At the very least, it seems like a weird way to relieve financial worries, since you, yourself, do not have enough money. You can easily come up with plenty of convincing reasons to forget about this harebrained idea called glad-giving. No matter. I urge you to take that initial plunge. You will never regret it.

Evaporating like dew...

The only thing left for you to do now is start. You have no excuse for delay. What do you need to start? Nothing. That's right—glad-giving operates on the basis of income, not assets or savings. You do not need to invest in supplies or materials before you are ready to begin. Everything you need, you already own. You don't need to have one penny set aside in order to start.

Even if you are unemployed, even if you are on welfare, even if you exist on handouts from others, you are ready for glad-giving. No matter what, you can practice this method exactly as I've described it, and it will work as effectively for you as anyone else.

> *"Plenty of people despise money, but few know how to give it away."*
> La Rochefoucauld

Everyone, no matter how destitute he or she is right now, no matter how dismal his or her financial situation is at this time, receives some income from somewhere. In other words, *everyone* has some cash coming in, no matter how little or how infrequently.

Let's look at an extreme case. Let's say you have no job and no paycheck. Let's say you are homeless and living under a bridge. You have no car, no telephone and no access to public services. Let's say you're lazy too. The only cash you ever see is an occasional handout from a stranger on the street. That averages about one dollar a week, just enough to buy a candy bar once in a while. That's perfect! Excellent! You're all set to start!

The next time someone hands you a dollar bill, before you spend it on food or anything else, you should automatically think *not* that you were handed one dollar, but that you were handed ninety-five cents. The nickel you deduct is earmarked for glad-giving. Immediately, take that nickel and give it away right then and there. Turn around and hand it to the hobo standing next to you if you need to, but give it away as soon as possible. Do it! And keep doing it consistently. Then watch what happens. Watch your life transform before your eyes.

When the results of glad-giving start happening, you may not believe the depth of change. Not only does money flow into your life, but your mental programming transforms. The way you view the world takes on a new and dynamic dimension. Your money addiction shifts to a preference, which reduces the force repelling money from you. Your money worries evaporate like dew in the morning sun. This transformation happens as you look on in wonder and gratitude. Do not say this cannot happen to you, because it can—and will.

Enjoying how...

There are so many benefits to a life of glad-giving that I could never describe them all in one book. In addition to creating abundance for yourself, you experience the joy of giving, one of the most profound pleasures a human being can feel. You've no doubt heard the old saying, "It is more blessed to give than to receive." By practicing glad-giving, you become one of the "rich folks" who get to have all the fun of giving. Before long, that old saying takes on a special meaning for you personally.

> *"You can't live a perfect day without doing*
> *something for someone who will never be*
> *able to repay you."*
> John Wooden

You may have noticed that I have said little in this chapter about glad-giving for the sake of helping others. Discussion has centered on what glad-giving does for you, the giver. Obviously, when you donate money to worthwhile causes, you are spreading goodwill and doing your part to contribute to a better world. That is good. Recognition of that fact is comforting and makes you feel good about yourself.

However, generosity, admirable as it is, is not the focus of this book. I am not attempting to mask underlying motivations, and I feel no compulsion to cloak glad-giving in a halo of glorious deeds and happy faces. People who practice glad-giving are honest about what they are doing. Most are logical, reasonable and pragmatic individuals acting with enlightened self-interest. They realize that their donations help good causes, but they also realize that being motivated by personal ambition is human nature and admirable in its own way.

Always be honest with yourself. Do not feel guilty for acknowledging that your first motivation is your own financial welfare, if that is the case. I mention all of this only to prepare you for thoughts you may have later.

After a while, you may realize that, with all the good you're doing, your motivation is based on your own desire for financial gain. You may feel uncomfortable with that thought, figuring that you are selfish or egocentric. Don't be hard on yourself. Whether you know it or not, your heart is in the right place.

There is nothing wrong with wanting personal success. You are entitled to prosperity and happiness. If that is the path that led you to glad-giving, so be it. If your glad-giving benefits the world, so much the better. But never feel less than honorable about your glad-giving, no matter what your motivation.

If you want to get rich, then get rich. If you feel good when you give to others, then enjoy how you feel. Just get out there and give some money away—and don't worry about whether or not your motivation is pure. You have nothing to worry about.

> *"If money is your God, it's going to hurt you too much to turn loose of it. The way I feel about those pieces of green paper is: you can't take them with you, but right now you can trade them in for pleasure, or to bring pleasure to other people. If God had wanted you to hold onto money, he'd have made it with handles."*
> "Treetop" Jack Straus

If you feel pumped up right now and ready to get started with glad-giving, then by all means, go. Remember this: glad-giving operates on the basis of income only, which means you do not need to possess any money whatsoever or touch any assets you've already saved. There is absolutely no reason not to begin glad-giving with the next chunk of money that comes your way.

In one last-ditch effort to talk yourself out of glad-giving, you may claim you cannot afford to do it. You may try to convince yourself that money is tight right now and you simply cannot afford it. I say, nonsense! The real question is: can you afford not to?

10

Your Life
of Abundance

THIS CHAPTER CONTAINS extra pointers to minimize
your repellant force. Like the chapter with extra pointers
for maximizing your attractive force, the suggestions
here are optional. You can follow them or not as you see
fit. If you apply a program of glad-giving to your life, no
matter what else you do or don't do, you will upgrade
your monetary addiction. The following suggestions,
however, can speed results and enhance your life of
abundance.

Be loose about money.

I do not mean you should be reckless. I mean you
should cultivate an attitude of carefreeness. Realize you
can get by without much money. Being poor may not be
what you prefer, but the world does not end if you
suddenly have to tighten your belt. Money is useful, but
it is not the most important thing in the world.

Speak cheerfully about your financial affairs. When discussing money with friends, be quick to say, "I'm not concerned about money anymore," or "I have plenty of money these days." Do not worry about trivial sums. Let the person at the cash register keep the change once in a while. Adopt the attitude that small amounts of money are insignificant to you. Treat money lightly, at least for outward appearances.

Again, don't be stupid or careless with money. Don't throw it away. Don't lose track of it. Don't flush it down the toilet. All you need to do, when dealing with money, is loosen up and relax.

Spend money.

I do not mean you should suddenly go on a wild spending spree. I mean you should be willing to part with money in order to buy whatever you want.

On occasion, you may find yourself debating whether or not to purchase a certain item. Chances are, you really do want the item or you would not waste time wrangling with yourself about it. Chances are, the main argument against buying the item is cost. In that case, buy it. When a buying decision is difficult, lean toward buying.

Do not construe this advice to mean you should intentionally increase your spending or go out and buy things you don't want. That's not what I am saying. This advice concerns only decisions involving an item you truly want. If you find yourself in doubt solely due to considerations of expense, then I recommend that you be willing to part with your money. This situation may occur infrequently, and this advice may have little long-range impact on your budget; but the willingness implicit in this attitude predisposes you to beneficial results.

Don't worry about debt.

I do not mean you should acquire a bunch of credit cards and run them to the limit without regard for consequences. What I mean is, you should feel at peace with being in debt if that is your current situation.

Many people live in debt. The United States government is the biggest deficit spender in history. Of course, the fact that a government does something does not make it wise policy, but it points out that debt is a fact of life in today's world. If, right now, you find yourself in debt, don't sweat it. You'll dig out eventually. If you slide a bit further into debt along the way, don't torment yourself. Being in debt, in and of itself, is no less honorable than anything else a person does in the world of finances.

Sure, debt is not your first choice. It's not something desirable, something you want to encourage in yourself. But, someday, all your debts will be a distant memory. In the meantime, chill out. Don't work yourself into a frenzy about something that's not even a problem of mismanagement. Anxiety compounds the problem. As long as you keep your level of debt manageable, your life will function smoothly. Nothing about your monetary situation will improve by adding worry to the equation.

Remember the child within.

I do not mean you should suddenly become immature and act irresponsibly. I mean you should remember the part of you that knows life is a game and sees money as a way to play.

Young children have almost no addiction to money. If they have a few dollars in their pocket, great. If not, that's cool too. Give a dollar to a three-year-old and watch what happens. The child celebrates the good fortune.

The youngster thanks you profusely and then runs around the house jumping and shouting with joy. Some people might say that's because the child is ignorant and does not know the value of a dollar. I say it's because the child carries no addiction to any particular outcome regarding money and, therefore, experiences feelings with immediacy and passion. Remember that you, too, have the capability to feel that same passion.

Be more childlike with money, more playful. That does not mean you should treat money disrespectfully; it means you should have more fun with it. Enjoy your quest for money as if it were a game, because it is. Get in touch with the child that still lives within you. Remember the way you felt as a child, and notice that a part of you is still capable of those feelings today. Do whatever you must do to reach your monetary goals, but don't lose sight of the child who is doing the doing.

Think of things other than money.

I do not mean you should never concern yourself with thoughts of money. I mean you should keep an awareness in the back of your mind that there are entire spheres of reality where money plays no part.

Normally, many of your waking hours are spent in thoughts related, in some way, to finances. A consciousness centered on money permeates nearly everything you think and do. You should remember that there are entire worlds, entire realities, not based on money. Think of love, sex, art, dance, music, poetry, prayer, meditation and others aspects of a fulfilling life. Money has no relevance when dealing with these experiences.

Someone once said to me, "Hey, man, in this day and age, it takes money to do those things." Obviously, money does make it easier for you to explore those areas. Money does give you greater access to the finer things in life. But that is beside the point. What I am suggesting is that you be aware of the existence of worlds that operate beyond money. They do exist. Think about them. Surely, you do not need any money to think about something. That too—the world of thought—is a universe apart from money.

You don't want money only for money's sake, do you? Of course not; green pieces of paper are of no value to you. You want money for what it can get you. Well, then, spend some time thinking about those things that money can get. Let your mind wander into thoughts of the wonderful treasures life has to offer.

In making this recommendation, I am not suggesting you change your behavior. An awareness of these worlds need not alter what you do in life. This awareness does, however, create the space for you to realize that money isn't everything. There are worlds without money that await you. Entire universes exist where money has no relevance whatsoever. Realize this. Become intimately aware of these realities. Ponder them. Enjoy these miraculous worlds. Take comfort in their existence—and their ultimate survival.

Don't worry too much about money. Get all the pleasure you can out of whatever comes your way, and enjoy what life has to offer. Kick back and have some fun. Come alive. You deserve it.

Creating the life...

Carl was in his early twenties when I met him. He was broke. He was living in a tiny studio and was being evicted because he could not pay the rent. But Carl's dismal situation did not stop him from obsessing about money. He spent virtually all his time in thoughts concerning money.

He would stay up late at night drawing charts and projecting his future riches. He read constantly about business plans and investment strategies. He was also well-read on all the latest positive-thinking techniques. To a casual observer, Carl looked the perfect picture of a man on the verge of financial triumph. Everyone who met Carl came away convinced he was a person destined to succeed.

Everyone was wrong. Carl went nowhere. Ten years later, he was still holed up in an apartment reading books about money. He went through two wives, two ulcers and dozens of business ideas.

One day Carl said to me, "I just don't understand it. Nothing I do ever works. I've tried everything. If something doesn't break for me soon, I'm going to lose it."

With that statement, his problem became obvious to me. Carl possessed a raging addiction to the idea of being successful. What everyone mistook for a positive attitude was actually a negative addiction to money. Carl feared failure. All his motivations were fear-based, a sure sign of addiction.

With a slow and steady voice, I asked him a question. "Carl, is it okay with you that you're broke?"

"Hell no!" he shouted. "I'd rather die!"

I looked him straight in the eye and said, "Carl, it seems to me you've been broke a long time. Maybe you're going to be broke for a while yet before you come out of this. Perhaps you should accept that fact and let it be alright for now. That's not so bad, you know. There are other things in life."

Those words must have triggered something inside him. He didn't reply; he just sat there thinking. That night, Carl wanted to go back to studying his books. I said no. I told him to set aside all his charts and money books and come with me to a rock concert. He did.

The next day, I started Carl on a program of glad-giving. I also told him to find some activity he could throw himself into. He took up bodybuilding. For the first time in his life, Carl became interested in something besides money. I guess he figured if he was going to be broke for a little while longer, he might as well do something productive in the meantime.

About a year later, I ran into Carl in a store. He looked great. Not only was his body massive, but he had a glow of confidence about him. His business was booming. He had a new car, a new house and a new girlfriend. He told me he was thrilled with life.

"Still worried about money?" I asked him.

"Not at all," he replied. Then he put his hand on my shoulder and said something I'll never forget. "You know, Victor," he said, "it's okay with me if I go broke. I've been broke before. Having money is great, but so what. I doubt I'll ever be broke again, but if I am, c'est la vie."

Carl had upgraded his money addiction to a preference. He still preferred to have money, obviously, but his desperate state of addiction was a thing of the past. Carl had reduced the force repelling money from his life. That allowed whatever else he did—whatever specific money plans he employed—to bring results.

True, not everyone has the same degree of addiction Carl had. But, no matter what amount of addiction you possess, that addiction is working behind the scenes to repel money from your life. Why not minimize it? Why not cut that force down to size so that whatever else you do can work to put money in your pocket?

You now know a way to do just that. Addiction is the culprit here. Free yourself from your addiction to money, and money will come your way. Without addiction breathing down your neck, you can start creating the life you want. Go ahead, lean back in your chair and let that lazy grin come across your face. Don't worry, wherever you're headed, it's going to be a grand and profitable adventure.

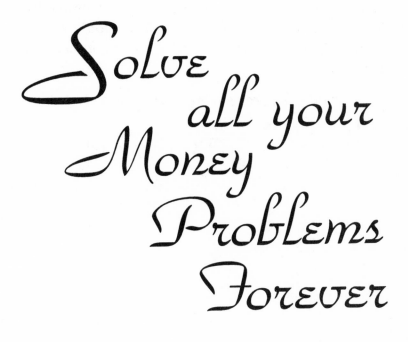

Solve all your Money Problems Forever

"The future is a mirror without any glass in it."

Xavier Forneret

11

The Two-Prong Method

THE INFORMATION IN THIS chapter is what this book is all about. The preceding pages were written to facilitate your understanding of this one chapter. Read it carefully, and give it your full attention.

Wielding full power...

You now know two vital laws of the universe. The Law of Attraction states that you attract the images you hold in your subconscious mind. The Law of Repulsion states that you repel what you are addicted to. These two concepts form the basis of an effective approach to creating a flow of money.

IMAGE $\Longrightarrow$ ATTRACTS

ADDICTION $\Longrightarrow$ REPELS

What you must incorporate into your life is what I call "the two-prong method." That is exactly what I have described in this book.

Your practice of glad-giving results in a state of consciousness with less monetary addiction, which results in a lessening of the force repelling money from your life. This decrease in repellant force "frees" money to come to you. At the same time, your affirmations implant the images you choose into your subconscious mind. This results in an increase in the force attracting money into your life.

In other words, your glad-giving releases money and frees it to flow in any direction. Your affirmations pick up from there and attract money in *your* direction. This is the essence of the two-prong method—the most powerful method that exists to create a positive flow of money into your life.

THE TWO-PRONG METHOD

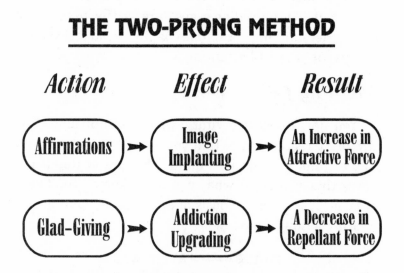

To solve all your money problems forever, practice the two-prong method. In other words, combine affirmations and glad-giving. To derive the full benefit, it is necessary that you do both parts, not just one.

You cannot know in advance if, in your case, only one of these techniques is sufficient to produce a flow of money. It may be. In many cases, however, doing only one of them does not generate massive results. You need the two parts working for you at the same time. By doing affirmations and glad-giving together, you wield the full power of the two-prong method.

Using both feet...

Let's examine how the two-prong method creates a flow of money into your life. Chances are, if you are like most people, you start out as illustrated below.

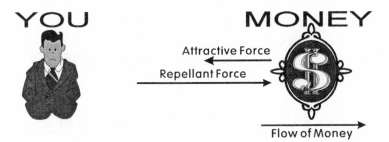

Notice that both your attractive force and your repellant force are present. As shown, your repellant force is greater than your attractive force. Thus, money tends to flow out of, rather than into, your life.

Let's suppose you decide to do only affirmations, and not glad-giving. This definitely increases your attractive force toward money. But, since you retain the same degree of monetary addiction, your repellant force remains unchanged. One of two things could happen. First, you could increase your attractive force, but not enough to overcome your unchanged repellant force. This situation is shown in the top figure on the next page.

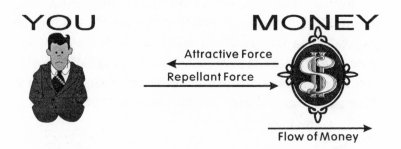

As you can see from the above figure, the flow of money remains out of your life. Although you have increased your attractive force, your repellant force is strong enough to offset the increase.

The second possible outcome of doing only affirmations occurs if your affirmations increase your attractive force to a level that is sufficient to overcome your unchanged repellant force. The figure below illustrates this situation.

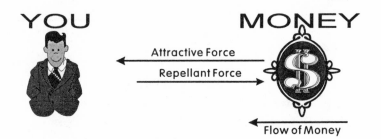

As you can see, the flow of money is now into your life. In this case, by doing only affirmations, you increase your attractive force enough to offset even a substantial repellant force. Keep in mind, there is no way to determine in advance which of these two outcomes you will get—that is, whether affirmations alone will increase your attractive force enough to overcome your unchanged repellant force.

Now, let's assume you decide to try only glad-giving, and not affirmations. Again, starting with the figure on page 203, one of two things could happen. First, you could decrease your repellant force, but not enough to drop below the strength of your unchanged attractive force. This situation is shown in the following figure.

Notice that you have reduced your repellant force, but not enough to allow your unchanged attractive force to win out. In this case, glad-giving, by itself, does not alter the flow of money.

The second possible outcome of doing only glad-giving is that you could reduce your repellant force to a level that is small enough to allow your unchanged attractive force to dominate. This is illustrated below.

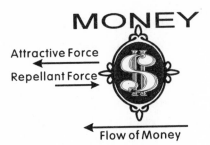

As shown, the flow of money is into your life. In this case, glad-giving alone is sufficient to reduce your repellant force to a strength less than your attractive force.

As you can see from the scenarios just presented, trying either affirmations or glad-giving, alone, may or may not be sufficient to produce results. There is no way to predict the outcome. If you try only one of these techniques, you may or may not derive noticeable benefit.

However, if you do both simultaneously, I am able to predict the outcome: The two-prong method will, unquestionably, create a flow of money in your direction. With the full power of the two-prong method working for you—both affirmations and glad-giving at the same time—you cannot fail. By doing both parts together, you simultaneously increase your attractive force and decrease your repellant force. The figure below illustrates the effectiveness of applying both affirmations and glad-giving in conjunction with each other.

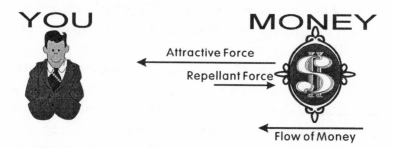

Compare this figure with the one on page 203. Notice that two things have happened. Your attractive force has increased and, at the same time, your repellant force has decreased. The result is a strong flow of money in your direction. Comparing these two figures illustrates the potency of the two-prong method.

When you were a baby, your mother did not teach you to walk using only one foot. Even though you could do that—you could hop around on one foot all your life— she knew that using both feet was a far more effective way to get where you want to go. Likewise, you may be able to generate a flow of money using only affirmations or glad-giving. It is possible for you to "hop around" with only one. However, using both techniques together is a far more effective way to get where you want to go.

Working in tandem...

If you practice affirmations, you attract money. If, at the same time, you are addicted to money, your attractive force needs to overcome your repellant force for you to see results. If your power of imagery is strong enough to generate an attractive force greater than your repellant force, then doing affirmations is sufficient, and money will come your way. If, however, your addiction to money is too great, affirmations may not be able to overcome your repellant force, at least not for a while.

An understanding of these two forces explains why "positive thinking," by itself, does not work for some people. They try it, they think and think and think until their head hurts, yet they do not get the results they seek. This is because all the while they are thinking positively, they remain addicted to money, producing a repellant force greater than the attractive force generated by their new attitude. Thus, money eludes them and they cannot understand why. These people end up convinced that positive thinking does not work.

This is where the other "prong" of this method comes in. Glad-giving frees you from your addiction to money, which minimizes your repellant force. Once your repellant force is lessened, affirmations can produce results. In other words, glad-giving sets the stage for your affirmations to do their thing. This two-prong method does two things at once. That's why it is so powerful.

Let me tell you about Scott. Scott was stubborn. He refused to do both affirmations and glad-giving at the same time. Scott would alternate. He would write affirmations for a few months, then he'd stop and donate money for a few months. Then he'd stop that and go back to writing affirmations. Scott actually had a measure of success doing this. Over a period of two and a half years, he secured a high-paying job with cable TV, got married and purchased a house. He felt reasonably content and was proud of his efforts.

One day I asked him, "Well, Scott, you've been doing this stuff for years now; have you solved all your money problems yet?"

"I'm doing quite well," he replied. "No complaints."

"I know," I said, "but have you totally eliminated all financial worries from your life? Have you?"

He thought about that for a while. Then he said, "Well, no. I have bills to pay. I have to worry just like everyone else does. There's lots of expenses."

I made a suggestion. "Scott, try your affirmations and glad-giving at the same time, say for six months. At the end of that time, if you still want to stop, then take a break from both of them. You owe it to yourself to try them both at the same time." He agreed.

A few months later, Scott invited me to meet him for lunch—at one of the finest restaurants in San Francisco. As soon as he saw me, he said, "So, this is how it feels!'

When he ordered a $100 bottle of Chablis, I felt compelled to ask him, "Can you afford that?"

He smiled and replied, "Hey, money is no problem for me anymore."

I knew exactly what he meant. Scott had discovered the power of using affirmations and glad-giving together.

Affirmations, alone, may work for you. But, just as likely, they may not produce the kind of mind-blowing results you want. They may need help. Glad-giving, alone, may work for you. But, again, it may not knock your socks off with results. It may need help. Now, put the two together. Combine affirmations and glad-giving—and look out! The two of them, working in tandem, cannot fail. The two-prong method will definitely generate a solid flow of money into your life.

Covering all the bases...

Maybe you think this two-prong method has nothing to do with the hard reality of day-to-day living. Maybe you think this method does not relate to the task of making money. Maybe you think this approach is based on superstition and cannot possibly have any effect on anything. If so, you are wrong. The two-prong method has everything to do with making money.

To say that money exists due to the creative power of the mind does not detract from the reality of it. Money is real. Drop your bank statement on your desk and listen to the sound it makes; that's reality. To say that money becomes manifest because of your subconscious mind does not, in any way, make money less real. This ethereal connection merely explains money's existence from a deeper perspective than that of the material world. The material world is an aspect of reality, and money is an aspect of the material world.

Throughout this book, I have focused on the concept of "forces" and their effect on the "flow of money." I have not discussed financial matters from the standpoint of getting jobs, saving money, pyramiding investments, buying real estate, playing the stock market or any specific ways of accumulating wealth. All these methods are good as far as they go. They all have their place and can be useful. Many individuals use a knowledge of these methods to pave their way to riches. However, many other individuals try these same methods and fail. Why is that? Why does one person try a plan and get rich and another person try the same plan and go broke? I'll tell you why. It's because money-making plans are only a surface solution to financial problems.

This book does not instruct you on career decisions or educate you about economic strategies. That is not an oversight on my part. I have intentionally avoided these subjects because the method I give operates at a much deeper level. Whatever specific jobs, investments or monetary plans you pursue are incidental. If you want to solve all your money problems forever, you must get to the root of your monetary situation. The most basic approach possible involves the flow of money as it relates to your life.

If the flow of money is out of your life, all the sound money advice in the world profits you little. High-paying jobs elude you; "sure" stocks go broke the moment you invest in them; "foolproof" money plans somehow manage to fail for you. Mysteriously, one bad break after another prevents you from reaching your goals.

On the other hand, once you create a flow of money into your life, money comes to you. Period. *How* is no problem. You get that job; you buy the right real estate; you win at the stock market. You can do no wrong. You find success around every corner. The things that happen to you seem amazing, but they happen nonetheless.

Whatever needs to happen for you to manifest money will happen—no matter what the odds, no matter what specific money-making plans you implement. Once your flow of money is established, money cannot help but come your way. It has to. The laws of physics guarantee it. You may as well relax and enjoy your journey to prosperity. Work whatever job you want; pursue whatever interests excite you; do whatever you feel like doing; and watch your financial worth skyrocket. And by all means, stop worrying!

Think of the energy you now expend trying to rearrange the situations in your life so you can achieve financial well-being and peace of mind. Meanwhile, your quest for security grows more elusive year after year. Since the people around you have similar struggles, you may have lowered your expectations and arrived at the conclusion that total financial freedom is not realistic for you. Baloney! The two-prong method allows you to achieve the highest imaginable level of wealth—as well as any other goal you truly desire.

Understand that I do not want you to *only* become rich. That may happen, but riches are not the primary concern here. You purchased this book in order to solve all your money problems forever. Implicit in that statement is a consciousness that is free from worry. When you eliminate your worry about money, you *directly* solve all your money problems forever.

I am not saying that affirmations will make you a billionaire. I am not saying that glad-giving will make you a billionaire. I am not even saying that both of them together will make you a billionaire. What I am saying is that this two-prong method will create a positive flow of money into your life. Once you've created a reliable flow of money, you have solved all your money problems forever. It's as simple as that.

To achieve any goal and have it endure, you must do two things: you must create a vivid image of your goal, and you must let go of your attachment to the goal. The two-prong method accomplishes both things. When you faithfully practice this method, you will succeed at whatever money-making activities you pursue.

Many people find my message of hope hard to accept when they first encounter it. "Prosperity can't be that easy," they reason. "There must be more to success than just this two-prong method; a prosperous person needs to know a great deal about monetary facts and figures; the attainment of wealth must be an uphill struggle for forty years." Wrong! Dead wrong! By applying this two-prong method, you solve all your money problems forever, and the transformation happens so quickly you are left wide-eyed in wonder.

Combining affirmations and glad-giving creates a powerful one-two punch that money cannot resist. The two-prong method covers all the bases. Affirmations work for some people. Glad-giving works for some people. Put them together and you can't miss. You've got the whole ball game now.

Beginning life anew...

The laws of the universe will prevail, regardless of what you do. If you decide to apply these laws to your life, you benefit. If you decide not to apply them, you have no one but yourself to blame for your continued financial turmoil. I am speaking to those of you who think you know it all, yet complain about your lot in life. I am speaking to those of you who refuse to face your doubts. If you feel you are too "sensible" to believe what I say, I feel sorry for you. More sad stories lie ahead for you.

On the other hand, to those of you who prefer to keep an open mind, I have the greatest of respect for you. To those of you who resolve to test the techniques I've put forth in these pages, I congratulate you. You will benefit. You will advance and prosper in all areas of life. You will find tremendous rewards coming your way at every turn. You will encounter a new consciousness, one that is free from worry and confusion. You will open the door to a new life, a life in harmony with all your ambitions.

Do not say you don't have enough money to implement this method, because you don't need any money. Do not say the method is too much work, because it's not any work. Do not say you can't afford the time, because there is no better way to spend a few minutes each day. Do not say the two-prong method is too complicated, because even a six-year old can do it—and has! Do not say you are totally content and want nothing more out of life, because you'd be kidding yourself. In fact, there is nothing you can say if you are looking for an excuse.

MOST PEOPLE ARE ALWAYS GETTING READY TO LIVE, BUT THEY NEVER REALLY LIVE.

Does the above statement ring true for you? If so, you need not wait one minute longer to start living. You can live now! You can start immediately on the road to your new life. You have no reason to delay.

Living in the moment is the way to happiness. Indeed, this one principle has been called the "secret" of happiness. *Now* is when you must accept a richer life. *Now* is when you must come to grips with what you want. *Now* is when you must decide to act. Not later. Now!

The time has come to change your life. The time to begin is this very moment. There will never be a better time, and getting started will never be any easier than it is right now. Now is the most precious moment there has ever been. Treasure this moment, for it marks the beginning of your new life. A new day is dawning for you, and the sun is shining brightly. Everything is looking up for you now. Thank God! You'll soon be free of your burdens. I know it makes you feel good to read this, because I feel good for writing it.

At this glorious moment, you are going to begin a new life—a life of ease and comfort, a life of joy and celebration. You will find the greatest of happiness and prosperity. This is no joke! Believe it! I know you will. I have faith in you.

THE BEST OF EVERYTHING TO YOU ALWAYS!

Questions
and Answers

THE FOLLOWING ARE SOME of the most frequently-asked questions about the material in this book. These questions are based on actual discussions and interviews conducted over several years. I hope this chapter answers any considerations that may come up for you.

Maximizing your attractive force...

Q... You say thoughts create reality. I've heard that before. But how do you know it's true? Is there any way to prove it?

A... Yes. There are many ways to prove it. The Law of Attraction is irrefutable and stands up to all investigative measures. In recent years, scientists have uncovered a wealth of evidence indicating that human thoughts exert a direct, physical influence on reality. Modern-day research makes a convincing case for the old adage: "Mind over matter."

Q... I'd like to believe that. But how can I prove it?

A... Forget the scientific evidence! For thousands of years, intuitive people have known that thoughts create reality. Eastern philosophies have taught this principle since the dawn of creation. I say forget that too. By far, the most convincing proof you can have is to test these ideas yourself. Try a program of affirmations. After that, you won't care whether science proves it or philosophy agrees. Change your thoughts at a subconscious level, and watch your life transform. Your entire world will change—things you didn't even think *could* change. Let that be your proof.

Q... What if I don't believe any of these theories?

A... You don't have to. If you choose not to accept the fact that your mind has the power to influence reality, that's fine. But, believe it or not, your subconscious mind does have that power. And you can use that power to your benefit.

Q... How does the subconscious mind create reality?

A... I don't know. I have to be honest with you; I don't know how it works. But I know it *does* work, and that's what I care about. Through a method unknown and incomprehensible to human logic, the subconscious mind draws upon the power of the universe to transmute images into their physical counterparts.

Your mind knows the secret process by which images are converted into reality. I don't know the details of this secret, and that's fine with me. I don't know how gravity works either, but I know it does. You do not need to know how this method works. All you need to know is that it does. Try it and you will see. I suggest that you accept this method the same way you accept medicine from your doctor without a scientific explanation of how it works.

Q... What if I don't want to do this stuff?

A... Fine. You are free to decide that you want no part of this. But I have news for you: you are already doing it, whether you know it or not, whether you like it or not. Maybe you have been imagining a lack of money, a lack of success, a lack of happiness. If you envision a life of struggle, that's exactly what you get. You are the creator of your world. Consciously or unconsciously, you are molding your destiny. For better or worse, you are constructing the scenery of the universe in which you live. The experiences you have in life are precisely the experiences you have imagined in your mind. The same thoughts you have been thinking subconsciously, you are now realizing in life.

Q... Is there any way to stop this from happening?

A... I'm afraid not. You can choose not to believe these concepts if you want, but, like it or not, facts are facts. Listen to me. What I'm divulging here is a law unknown to most people. This law has always held true for you, either for good or for bad. Look around you. How is your life going? Whatever answer you give to that question, your life right now is the result of your thoughts. The reason things are the way they are rests with the images you hold in your subconscious mind. You have no reason to be afraid of that fact. Knowledge of how things work empowers you. You can use this knowledge to your advantage. It's there for the using.

Q... Are affirmations effective?

A... You bet they are! Affirmations are the most effective way known to reprogram the subconscious mind. And the subconscious mind is the only way to go. All other methods, if they work at all, are effective only insofar as they are able to influence the inner workings of the mind.

Q... Other money-making methods can work too, can't they?

A... Sure. But only if your mind lets them. Suppose you try a real-estate plan and eventually succeed at making money. Truth is, the credit for success rests with your subconscious mind. The real-estate plan sounded good enough that it allowed you to believe—subconsciously— that you would get rich. The outward appearance is that the real-estate plan created your wealth. This view is flawed, however, since others have, no doubt, tried the same plan and failed. To succeed, you must expect success at the subconscious level. Affirmations are the most effective method known to reach and influence your elusive subconscious mind.

Q... Do I need to believe affirmations will work in order for them to work?

A... Nope. Just do the program anyway. Affirmations are different from other methods that require you to possess faith as the initial step.

Other methods say, "Believe first. All else will follow."

The natural reply is, "How do I make myself believe? How do I conjure up the required faith?" I have never heard a satisfactory answer to that question.

By contrast, I say, "Do affirmations first, and all else will follow."

That's the beauty of affirmations: once you start doing them, you experience results. After that, belief comes naturally. Before long, the question of faith will be a moot point.

Q... How many affirmations should I have at one time?

A... That, of course, is entirely up to you. Whatever you feel comfortable with is okay. Experience has shown that, for most people, an effective and manageable number is anywhere from one to ten.

Q... Should I change my affirmations regularly?

A... You *will* change your affirmations, whether you initially intend to or not. Modifying your affirmations is normal; allow it to happen.

Tim wanted to lose weight. He weighed 240 pounds when I told him about affirmations. That day, I asked him what he considered his ideal weight. He replied, 190 pounds. I suggested he write an affirmation declaring his weight at 190 pounds. He protested. He insisted that 190 pounds was unreasonable. He wanted to start with something within reach, such as 220. He didn't want to become discouraged if he failed to reach his goal. Even though I told him anything was possible, Tim was skeptical. So, he started with an affirmation for 220 pounds.

Tim lost weight so quickly that, within one month, he revised his affirmation to read, "I, Tim, now weigh 200 pounds." When he reached the 200-pound mark, he again revised his affirmation for 190 pounds. This, too, he achieved.

Tim then realized that even his original estimate of ideal weight was tempered by negative views of what he thought was reasonable to achieve. He discovered that his *true* ideal weight was 175 pounds. He composed a new affirmation. Today, Tim weighs 165 pounds, and he is concentrating on other areas of his life.

Q... Why don't you tell me *your* affirmations? Why can't I just use the same ones you used?

A... Because everyone is different, and everyone's desires are different. *You* are different. Even general desires such as "wealth" and "success" should be expressed in detail that is distinct for you. Part of this method's effectiveness comes from the fact that it forces you to examine yourself and uncover what you want. You need to determine, in detail, exactly what you, as a unique human being, want in your life.

Appendix A contains a list of sample affirmations. Keep in mind that this list is intended only as a reference to give you ideas as you formulate your own. Under no circumstances should you take an affirmation from this list and use it word for word.

Q... Why must I do affirmations? Why can't I just think positively?

A... Remember, your objective is to control the images implanted in your subconscious mind. The technique of writing and speaking affirmations is the most effective way known to do that.

Can you "think positively" at the subconscious level? I seriously doubt it. If you can, you have more ability than I or anyone else I know. Maybe you can think positively at the conscious level, but that's not good enough.

Your conscious mind knows how to fool you, how to give the appearance of change while your subconscious mind remains stuck in its rut. Affirmations are the surest way to directly affect your subconscious mind.

Q... I feel silly doing this stuff, reading to myself, writing the same thing over and over. What can I do about this feeling?

A... Nothing. Just keep reading and writing your affirmations anyway.

Remember Tim? He went from 240 pounds to 165 pounds using affirmations. This feeling of silliness was a major issue for him in the beginning. He was a macho man, and he felt ridiculous reading his affirmations to himself every day. But, silly or not, he did it anyway. That was then and this is now. Now, when I see the confidence in his eyes, I don't need to ask, "Hey, Tim, do you still feel silly?" Believe me, he doesn't.

I know you feel silly at first. That's normal. You do not yet believe this technique will work. But it will. Hang in there. I know of nothing that cures feeling silly, other than a little success. The feeling will pass.

Q... You say if a person expects something, it will happen. But sometimes I expect an outcome and something else happens. I get surprised. How can that be?

A... There is a difference between what you expect consciously and what you expect subconsciously. Only images implanted in your subconscious mind—images that lead to subconscious expectations—are the ones that become manifest. Usually, you don't even know what these subconscious expectations are; they can be different from your conscious expectations.

Let's say you are playing baseball and it is your turn to bat. You expect to get a hit. You've gotten a hit your last six at bats, and you can visualize yourself getting a hit. You just "know" you are going to clobber the ball. Instead, you strike out. Your mouth drops open in shock as you walk back to the dugout. How can this happen?

Simple. Your subconscious mind expected a strike out. Your conscious mind expected a hit, but hidden in your subconscious, unknown to you, was an image of you striking out. Even though you expected a hit consciously, your subconscious mind expected something different. What your subconscious mind expects is what you get. There is no exception to this rule.

Most of the time, you do not know what your subconscious mind expects or how to control that expectation. That is why affirmations are so powerful. They bypass the conscious mind and act directly on the subconscious.

Q... How do I know if the images I want are getting implanted into my subconscious mind?

A... The only way to know is by judging results. You cannot know by examining yourself or testing your subconscious mind. Watch for positive changes. When your life transforms right before your eyes, you will know.

Q... You say I should act like I'm already successful. You say I should pretend to be rich. Isn't that just a big lie? Isn't that being a fake?

A... Only at first. The way you act and the way you think are interrelated. The message of your actions sinks into your subconscious mind. In a short time, you actually *are* what you act. After that, your behavior is no longer an act. Besides, all your life, you've been acting, anyway;

the only difference is you've probably been acting poor. If you must act *some* way, it might as well be rich, right? If your behavior is an act, so be it. I ask you, who is harmed by your act?

Q... Isn't this whole method just positive thinking?

A... Certainly not. As I said before, a discipline of affirmations goes far beyond mere positive thinking. Affirmations get to the deepest and most personal levels of your subconscious mind. You can think positively all you like, but you may find your life remains unchanged.

Positive thinking is often not enough to produce the kind of dynamic results you want. This is because you are the sum of all your thoughts. Old thoughts continue to influence your life long after you no longer consciously think them. All the positive thinking in the world does not deal with the deep levels of mind where this programming resides. Affirmations do. Somehow, some way, a daily practice of affirmations gets to the root of what is holding you back. Affirmations attack at the source.

Q... Positive thinking works for a lot of people. Why are you putting it down?

A... I am not putting it down. I am only pointing out its limitations. Positive thinking is fine, as far as it goes. Positive thinking says: *Do you feel inferior? Do you think of yourself as a failure? Do you believe you are hopelessly stuck in a rut of poverty? Then change your thinking. Think you are successful. Think you are rich. Think positive!*

But how? Positive thinking does not say how! If you have the ability to think positively by sheer force of will, fine. If not, you're stuck.

Suppose you say to yourself, "I am rich." And your mind replies, "Like hell you are, you dimwit!" How do you counter that? How do you alter your thinking at the subconscious level? That is where positive thinking ends and affirmations begin. Through repetition of your affirmations, you get into your subconscious mind and produce results far more dramatic than you do with positive thinking. Affirmations go deep.

Minimizing your repellant force...

Q... You say I should free myself from addiction to money. Isn't that the same as not caring about money?

A... Definitely not. You can still care about money and continue to pursue your monetary goals in whatever manner you choose. Nothing needs to change outwardly. The only difference is that you upgrade your addiction to a preference. You adopt the attitude that whatever happens, everything is okay. Glad-giving is a surefire way to achieve this shift in attitude.

Q... Can't I just fake it? Can't I just declare I'm no longer addicted to money?

A... No. There is no faking it. You must feel this way legitimately, deep inside your mind. The mechanisms involved are subtle and respond only to sincere feelings.

Q... Are there any other ways, besides glad-giving, to obtain this freedom from addiction?

A... Quite honestly, there are. Many Eastern religions subject followers to severe disciplines that have the effect of loosening an addictive mind-set. Hypnosis, meditation and other introspective practices can also achieve this. Some Native Americans performed grueling exercises that had similar effects. But of all these techniques, glad-giving is, by far, the easiest and most direct method of attacking addiction—and it deals specifically with the addiction to money.

Q... I can see where glad-giving might make me feel better. But I can't, for the life of me, see what it has to do with solving my money problems.

A... I know. Glad-giving seems like a paradox at first. A woman once said to me, "Giving away money is supposed to solve my money problems? That's the most ridiculous thing I ever heard!" And so she went on her merry way, struggling to maintain her middle-class lifestyle. Last I heard, she filed for bankruptcy.

The apparent paradox of glad-giving is precisely the reason why most people who hear of this method ignore it. Glad-giving does not "make sense" to them. Personally, I don't care. I have given you, to the best of my ability, a basic understanding of this method. I have explained how glad-giving upgrades your monetary addiction to a preference, and how doing so releases money to flow your way. I can do no more. Either you recognize the value of what glad-giving is all about or you don't.

Try it, and you will know for yourself that it works. Then, the next time someone comes to *you* and says that glad-giving doesn't make sense, you'll find yourself in the same boat I am in now, trying to explain this apparent contradiction. You'll end up saying something like, "I understand, but...uh...well..."

Let me know if you think of anything better than that to say.

Q... You say I should give 1 to 5 percent of my income. But if 1 percent works fine, why on earth would anyone choose to give 5 percent?

A... Believe it or not, some people do. I suggest that, when you start, you begin at the low end of this range, with 1 percent. That's not much. If your take-home pay is $4000 a month, that's only $40 to give away. Some people have such kind hearts and feel so joyful once they start contributing to good causes that they cannot help increasing this amount. You decide for yourself. If you give 5 percent, fine. If you give 1 percent, that's fine too. Either way, your generosity speaks highly of you.

Q... It seems like giving away money is bad money management. Don't you agree?

A... Let me tell you a story. During my years as a professional poker player, I had the privilege of knowing Jack Straus, one fine human being. Jack won the World Series tournament in 1982, six years before his death.

One day Jack was in tax court. The IRS claimed he owed three million dollars in back taxes. While sitting in court waiting for his case to be called, Jack was watching the case ahead of his, a woman who owed $35,000. As a single mother whose husband had died, she could not afford her tax bill. The government was taking her home and possessions. She cried and pleaded. Suddenly, Jack stood up in the back of the courtroom and shouted, "Your honor, stick it on my tab!" Just like that, Jack gave thousands of dollars to a total stranger because he felt sorry for her.

Was that bad money management? Some would say so. Was he careless or irresponsible? Definitely not! Jack knew what he was doing.

At the poker table, Jack was ruthless. He played aggressively, fighting for every dollar. Other times, he spent money freely and compassionately. He knew when to be tight and when to be generous.

Glad-giving is not reckless. It is a discipline requiring control and fortitude. Yes, from the viewpoint of your accountant, glad-giving can be seen as unwise money management. But so what. If the end result is greater affluence and a life of serenity, who cares? Fact is, glad-giving is the smartest way possible to manage money.

Q... Is it better to give to individuals or to groups?

A... It makes no difference whatsoever as far as the effectiveness of this method is concerned. Giving to an individual is sometimes easier and more convenient, and you get to see the look on the person's face. But don't get sloppy. For example, do not count as glad-giving the allowance you give your children. If you take your nephew to the County Fair and you buy him a few rides, do not count the cost as glad-giving, especially if you would have done that anyway. When giving to individuals, you need to judge what constitutes glad-giving. When giving to organizations, the matter is usually cut-and-dried; you write the check, send it in and that's that. Deciding what part of your glad-giving should go to individuals and what part should go to organizations is a matter of personal preference. Do whatever you like.

Q... If someone owes me money, can I release them from repayment and count that as glad-giving?

A... That depends. You need to make a judgment on whether you think you would have gotten repaid. Let's say someone owes you $10,000 from fifteen years ago.

He has never repaid any of it, and he is now flat broke and dying of a terminal illness. You go to his deathbed and tell him to forget the debt. Can you then count that $10,000 as glad-giving—and figure you're paid up on your donations for the next dozen years or so? I say no, because you never would have gotten your money back from that person anyway.

Let's say someone owes you money and pays a set amount every month. You tell him to forget the next three payments. Can you count that as glad-giving? I say okay, because you are essentially giving him money that exists for you. In general, I do not recommend this practice as a way to conduct glad-giving, but from a technical point of view, it's acceptable.

Q... Isn't glad-giving religious?

A... Not at all. I prefer to divorce glad-giving from any connection with religion. If you are comfortable with a religious connotation, fine; but most people who practice glad-giving do so on the basis of scientific merit. True, religions teach the value of giving. I am aware of similarities between glad-giving and religious doctrine. But religion is not the issue here. Money is. Besides, benevolence and goodwill cut across all religious boundaries.

Q... If I already tithe 10 percent, do I now need to give an additional 1 to 5 percent to do glad-giving?

A... No. Your tithing counts as glad-giving. You are already giving more than you need to.

Q... It doesn't seem right for me to be donating to charities. I've always thought of rich people doing that. What if I'm not in a position to be giving away money?

A... You just cited a fantastic reason why you *should* give. If you think of rich people as the ones who donate money, then, when you practice glad-giving, you are acting rich, right? Think of yourself as one of those affluent people who can afford to make charitable donations and help fix the world's problems. You are in good company. You're a philanthropist now.

Q... What if I cannot afford to do glad-giving?

A... You can. You do not need any money at all to start a program of glad-giving. No matter how little money you have coming in, you have all you need to begin. Even on a fixed income, you can surely afford a measly 1 percent of your net. The claim that you cannot afford glad-giving is an excuse. Recognize it as such. It's up to you if you want to invent excuses; you are the one who must live with the choices you make. You are free to decide you want nothing to do with glad-giving. That's fine. But don't say you cannot afford it. That is not true. If you want to start a program of glad-giving, you can—and will. And the future will lie down before you like a welcome mat.

Solving your money problems...

Q... If I write affirmations for money, won't that increase my addiction to money? Isn't there a conflict here? Doesn't desire lead to addiction?

A... Not at all. An addiction is vastly different from a preference. You can tell when you upgrade an addiction to a preference because you become alright with the idea of not getting what you want. Ironically, once you make this transition, your desires become easier to attain.

Here's an important point: writing an affirmation for something you prefer does not increase your addiction to it. Your affirmation in no way contributes to addiction. Likewise, upgrading an addiction to a preference in no way precludes you from writing an affirmation. If you prefer something, affirmations make it happen. An affirmation and an addiction function independently.

Q... Could you go over the difference between an affirmation and an addiction one more time?

A... An affirmation is positive. An affirmation promotes confidence, allowing you to visualize something and know you can obtain it. An addiction is negative. An addiction invites worry, causing you to fear not obtaining something or fear losing it if you do obtain it. With addiction, you experience constant agitation because you believe you cannot live without the object of your desire. There is a fundamental difference between a person practicing affirmations, implanting positive images, and a person under the influence of addiction, suffering in fear.

Q... What about expectation? You say I should expect success. Isn't expectation like addiction?

A... No. When you expect something favorable, you nurture a positive outlook. Expectation fosters hope and promise. With a smiling heart, you look forward to better days. When you have an addiction to something, you want the item out of a sense of fear. You dread the future because you might not get what you think you need. And if you don't get it, all hell breaks loose. With an attitude of expectation, if you don't get what you want, everything is okay. Merely expecting something does not mean you go ballistic if you don't get it. Being addicted does.

Q... What if I don't want to do both affirmations and glad-giving. Which one of the two is better?

A... Some people insist on doing only one of these techniques, not both. I'm not sure why they feel that way, but they do. If you are a person who absolutely refuses to try both methods, then I suggest you try a program of affirmations first. Realize, however, that if affirmations don't do the trick, then you must add glad-giving to your program. Understand, too, that I cannot predict the degree of results you will get with either of these methods alone. Use them together, however, and I unabashedly guarantee results that'll blow you away.

Q... Isn't doing only one of these techniques better than doing none?

A... Yes. However, doing only one may not be enough to produce the kind of results you're after. You want good results, right? Otherwise, why bother? What you are trying to do here is implant an image into your subconscious mind and, at the same time, relinquish your attachment to the outcome. That's a tricky proposition. You need both parts of the two-prong method to assure success. One part alone is better than nothing, but both parts together are required for full throttle. I wish I could say otherwise. I wish I could make this even easier for you. But I can't. Besides, it's already easy enough.

Q... Where will I find the energy to do this method?

A... You already have it. What you need to do is get your energy in focus. You've already been expending huge amounts of energy in worry and negative emotions. Apply that same energy to your affirmations and glad-giving.

Energy is one thing you never run short of, because this method doesn't take much of it. The critical factor here is not energy, but initiative. If you must force yourself to get started, do it. The rest will follow.

Q... How long does this method take to work?

A... The answer to that question depends on many factors. How negative are your subconscious images? How great is your addiction to money? How long did you take to develop your current predicament?

Your negative images have been rooted in your mind for a long time, perhaps an entire lifetime. Be patient. Some time may be required to get them replaced. Likewise, your addiction did not spring up overnight. Allow some time to undo it.

Rather than answering this question in a vague way, saying that the time required "depends," I want to give you an answer that is as specific as possible. Anywhere from ten days to three months is usually sufficient time to see some discernible results. The first signs of success often appear sooner than you anticipate. One thing is certain: no matter how long it takes, results happen when they should. Keep in mind that a program of affirmations and glad-giving is a lot less time-consuming than any other method known. And I have never seen this two-prong method fail when the person used it properly and stuck with it. Never! That's a pretty good record.

Q... It can't really be that easy, can it? Just give away a little of my income, read and write my affirmations, and that's it?

A... Yes. It is exactly that easy, and that's all there is to it. The two-prong method is all you need to know.

Q... If all you say is true, and it's so doggone easy, then why aren't more people doing it?

A... There are many reasons why certain people are not interested in the two-prong method. Perhaps the main reason is that they feel silly doing it. They feel embarrassed at the thought of what others might think. Many people feel they lower themselves to try something that is out of the ordinary. Simply put, most people never try the two-prong method because they are stuck in old patterns. Few people have the courage to break free.

Realize that the reason a minority of the population uses the two-prong method is not because the method doesn't work, but because few ever try it. You may reason that if this method is so great, then word would get out and someone would surely tell you about it. Well, what do you think is happening here? Here I am telling you about it! *It works!* There, I just told you about it. For heaven sakes, don't let anything prevent you from trying this method. If you can rise above silly doubts, then go for it. Be one of the minority of successful people. To heck with the majority, who outright refuse success.

Q... I'm not getting any younger. At what age is it too late to start this method?

A... It is never too late. No matter what your age, you have more than enough time to turn your life around and begin to live fully. No matter who you are, no matter what your sex, social status or political persuasion, this method is your cup of tea. Hear my words. I know you enjoy reading these words of hope. I know you want to believe what I say. Then go ahead and believe. Go ahead and take hold of your future. Start now to repair your life. The world is waiting for you.

Q... What if I'm already wealthy? I don't need this method then, do I?

A... You never "need" this method. This two-prong method is simply a tool that exists if you want to use it. It is a proven method of generating a flow of money into your life. If that interests you, fine. If not, fine too.

Keep in mind, however, that even if you already are making money, you could be making more. If you already are rich, you could be richer. If you already have money flowing into your life, you could still increase the rate of flow. If you'd rather not do those things, no problem. It's your choice.

Q... What if everyone did this method? We can't all be rich, can we?

A... Says who? Let's look at each part of the two-prong method. If we all did affirmations, we'd all have what we want. I see no problem with that. Since we all express our desires differently, no one would object to anyone else's success. If everyone were prosperous, we'd have a world of content people.

If everyone practiced glad-giving, we'd experience a subtle redistribution of wealth. What a beautiful way to achieve economic parity—voluntarily, without government interference! If glad-giving became commonplace, a percentage of resources would gradually drift down to the low-income strata of society. Without legislation, we'd have welfare reform that would please us all. What if everyone did this method, you ask? My answer: That would be great. We'd have heaven on earth.

Q... We'll never see that kind of change, will we? That can't happen, can it?

A... There's that word again, *can't!* That word was first uttered by an old caveman when his son set out to invent the wheel. It was later used by renowned thinkers of the day when Henry Ford built his factory. We heard it again when Orville and Wilbur wanted to get off the ground. And again when Mr. Einstein said we could harness energy from atoms. Need I say more? I guarantee you, change will occur! It is up to you to direct the tides of that change. Whether your life changes for better or worse is your province. Since you are the architect of your destiny, you can steer the future wherever you want. Instead of sitting around saying *can't*, stand up and use the power you hold within you.

Q... This method seems rather self-centered. What about helping others? Shouldn't I strive to be rich for the good that I can then do for people less fortunate?

A... Doing good for others is, of course, admirable. But, please, do not use this reasoning as a weak rationalization for attaining wealth, as though you do not deserve riches by merit of your own worth. You *do* deserve riches. You deserve everything wonderful that life has to offer. It is right and proper for you to be wealthy.

From the tone of your question, I sense guilt about desiring personal wealth. Perhaps you feel you are being selfish or dishonorable. You are not. You *should* want to be rich. Abundance is your birthright. You are entitled to prosperity. Money is good for you.

Q... But isn't money bad? Isn't it the source of evil?

A... People often say, "Money is the root of all evil." Actually, the correct Biblical quotation is: "The *love* of money is the root of all evil." For our purposes, "love of money" translates into "addiction to money." Addiction is what causes the trouble. Money, itself, is neither good nor bad.

Most people are taught they should take whatever is given them and desire nothing more. But that is an unnatural attitude. Everyone has a yearning for something better. You can suppress that desire and carry on in a state of semi-resolution, or you can recognize that you want a better life and take action to attain it. The latter approach is the one that leads to satisfaction. Do not be afraid of your yearning for financial freedom. Do not deny it. Do not feel selfish. Do not feel guilty. You have that yearning for a reason, a good reason. Hear your desire and act on it.

Q... Why did you write this book about money? Money isn't everything, you know.

A... True. There are more important things in life than money. But millions upon millions of men and women feel helpless, paralyzed by their preoccupation with money. They cannot consider other interests until they first get their finances straightened out. That is why the focus of this book is money.

Imagine you are reading a great book about chess. Suddenly, you stop and realize that chess isn't everything. Although that's true, chess happens to be the subject of that particular book. There are other more worthwhile things in life than chess, but if you are interested in chess, that book is a good book. Well, if you are interested in money, this book is a good book. Money isn't everything, but it happens to be the subject of this book.

In case you didn't notice, however, this book is not *only* about money. You can apply these principles to anything. Your affirmations can be used to produce any conceivable object, quality or situation you desire. Your glad-giving can be used to contribute positive energy to the betterment of the world. The very least you can do with the information in this book is solve all your money problems forever.

Q... I knew a guy who read a money-making book. He did what it said and nothing happened. How come?

A... That book was nothing like this one. To my knowledge, this is the only book ever written that combines these two techniques—affirmations and glad-giving. Some books may give you part of the equation. This one gives you the full scoop.

Q... Your book seems materialistic—talking about the things you can get. It's all me, me, me. Money doesn't buy happiness. Do you think it does?

A... No. But a release from money worries can free you to pursue happiness in whatever way you choose. For some people, money is a curse; for others, a blessing. Which it is in your case depends on you, on how you relate to it and how you use it.

I admit, this book is unlike others. There are plenty of books around to help you cultivate an attitude of acceptance and inner peace, that teach you to find contentment in a lower standard of living, that show the way to spiritual fulfillment without focusing on money. This book is not one of them. While those ideas are valuable, they are not the scope of this material. Besides, if you practice the two-prong method, those same realizations will come to you in time. Eventually, you will arrive at a spiritual place on your own.

I once had a lengthy discussion with a man about this topic. For hours, we debated the value of money and whether it helped or hindered one's quest for happiness. I remember at one point he pounded his fist on the table and shouted, "I just want the chance to prove that money doesn't buy happiness!" Well said. This book will enable you to discover that fact for yourself, if you want to.

Q... Why did you write this book? Be honest now.

A... A long time ago, a man told me about some of the principles in this book. That encounter changed my life; nothing has been the same for me since. I remain eternally grateful to him. Even though he died some time ago, he will forever occupy a special place in my heart.

I want to share with you what I know. Maybe this book represents your first encounter with these ideas. If so, maybe one day I will occupy the same place in your heart that this man does in mine. Perhaps, due to my writing this book, you will try the two-prong method. If I am responsible for the improved livelihood of just one human being, then writing this book was worth the effort. If this book results in a little less grief for our troubled planet, then so much the better.

Imagine what our world would be like if a sizeable percentage of people suddenly had no more money worries. What would that do to the crime rate? What effect would that have on poverty, inflation, unemployment and the global economy? Imagine such a world, if you can.

You see, I want you to be wealthy. I want you to be happy. I want everyone to be happy. Call me a dreamer if you must, but I always set my goals rather high. Hopefully, you do too.

13

Do It

READING A BOOK ABOUT something does not constitute proof of what is said. Only by applying what you read will you know if something works. The proof is in the pudding, so to speak. All the reasoning in the world carries little weight compared to results. Now is the time for you to try the two-prong method and know it works. The only way to prove it is to try it. I sure hope you do.

> *"On the day of judgment, we shall not be asked what we have read, but what we have done."*
> Thomas à Kempis

I know you can come up with excuses. I know you can cite "logic" to say the material in this book cannot be true. I don't care. Just do as I say, and all your "logic" will fly right out the window. I cannot stress this point strongly enough. Do it! Do it, and you will see for yourself. You cannot evaluate what I say unless you try it.

You may decide not to try this method. That's up to you. But let any claims of proof stop there. Do not say this method does or does not work until you know. If you want to evaluate it, try it. Do as I say, and you will solve all your money problems forever. That's the truth.

"Nothing will ever be attempted, if all possible objections must first be overcome."
Samuel Johnson

I have opened a door for you. It is a door that leads to a life forever free from financial worries. But you need to pass through that door. I urge you to take that important first step. Don't put it off. Delaying is flirting with disaster. If you wait too long, your enthusiasm will fade and you will blow it. Act now and the future is yours. It's that simple.

If you begin now, you will soon taste your new life. The metaphysical theory, the scientific explanation, the glowing testimonials don't mean squat. Convince yourself first. The only way to do that is to try the method and find out what happens. Don't just read what someone else has written on the subject, as you are doing right now. Know for yourself it works. Try it, and you will see.

"If you want to play the game and win, you've got to play 'full out.' You've got to be willing to feel stupid, and you've got to be willing to try things that might not work."
Tony Robbins

You now have a choice. You can decide to do nothing with the information you just read and go on with your life as before. Or, you can decide to put the two-prong method into action. Or...perhaps there is even a third choice: you can make no decision whatsoever and linger in limbo. If that is what you do, maybe my words will stick with you. Maybe you'll be unable to get that nagging, unsettled feeling out of your mind, the feeling that you should be doing something about this. Maybe at some later date, possibly years from now, you will be unable to endure that feeling of irresolution eating away at you. Maybe then, you will give this method a try, even if only to put the matter to rest once and for all.

If you decide not to try the two-prong method at this time, I suggest you hang on to this book and store it someplace safe. You never know whether, someday in desperation, you might dig it up and read it again. And you'd better have it handy.

"The great dividing line between success and failure can be stated in five words: I did not have time."
Henry Davenport

Give the two-prong method a try—and you are in for the surprise of your life! I am so excited for you! I almost wish that I could grab your hand and *make* you do this method. Then you'd see! Of course, I say this only to illustrate a point. I don't really want to force you to do anything. You have a free will of your own, and that is as it should be. All I can do is present the facts and let it go at that. What you do afterwards is your business.

I realize that you may read this book and never take action. I sit here wondering how I can persuade you to try this method. Then I realize, I cannot. The decision to act rests with you, alone. All I can do is trust—trust that you will make the decision that is right for you. I am confident you will.

Aren't you at least a little curious? Don't you want to know if any of this stuff is true? Well, the only way you will ever know is to try it.

PUT IT TO THE TEST!

If you are skeptical, I don't blame you. Skepticism is a sign of a healthy and inquisitive mind. Let your natural instincts guide you to check out the principles in this book and see what's up.

Regardless of what your feelings are at this moment, you owe it to yourself to test the two-prong method. I urge you with all my heart to go for it. If I'm wrong, you lose nothing. But what if I'm right?

> *"There comes a time when the risk to remain*
> *tight in a bud is more painful than the risk*
> *it takes to blossom."*
> Anais Nin

No matter what you decide to do with the information in this book, you must admit I have given you something of immense value, something of far-reaching proportions. Certainly, that has been worth the time you have invested in reading this.

I have shown you the way to a life that is free from financial worries. I implore you to reach out and take the prize that awaits you. If you do as I suggest, you will hardly be the same person a year from now. You will be wealthier and happier. I have kept my part of the bargain. The rest is up to you.

APPENDIX A
AFFIRMATIONS REFERENCE

THE FOLLOWING IS A LIST of general affirmations. However, I must emphasize: do *not* take your affirmations directly from this list. These affirmations are not intended to be used as is, but are intended only as a reference to give you ideas as you formulate your own.

Remember, using an affirmation written by someone else is never as effective as one you create yourself. Therefore, if you want to use one of these affirmations, rewrite it first. Change a few words and make it specific to you. Once it is yours, use it along with others you create.

If you are able to come up with plenty of affirmations on your own, then you have no need for this list. If that is the case, then don't use it. This list is here only if you need it for ideas. If you don't need it, then forget it. You don't miss a thing if you don't use this list.

The affirmations start on the next page. They are grouped into categories according to their focus. The blank line in each affirmation represents your name.

MONEY

I, _____, *have a $500,000 bank balance.*

I, _____, *experience money coming into my life every day.*

I, _____, *have $1,000,000 worth of assets.*

I, _____, *create money quickly and easily.*

I, _____, *am free of my addiction to money.*

I, _____, *earn $500,000 per year.*

I, _____, *make wise and profitable investments.*

I, _____, *attract money doing what I want.*

I, _____, *save $5,000 every month.*

I, _____, *have a consciousness free from money worries.*

POSSESSIONS

I, _____, *own a new red BMW 840.*

I, _____, *wear a pink St. John sequined gown.*

I, _____, *own 10 acres of prime Rancho Villa property outside Phoenix.*

I, _____, *watch television on a 52-inch SONY big-screen.*

I, _____, *own an IBM personal computer system with 9 gig hard disk and CD-ROM.*

I, _____, *have a freezer full of prime rib.*

I, _____, *sail every Sunday on my 24-foot boat.*

I, _____, *have building permits to develop the Danville property.*

I, _____, *keep everything I own in good working order.*

I, _____, *have money to purchase whatever I want.*

CAREER

I, _____, *love my work.*

I, _____, *have a career where I am admired by coworkers.*

I, _____, *am successful at my own desktop-publishing business.*

I, _____, *have received a $20,000 pay raise.*

I, _____, *work at Meyer & Associates as chief data technician.*

I, _____, *go to work with a smile on my face.*

I, _____, *have a job in which I help people.*

I, _____, *work only twenty hours a week.*

I, _____, *have written a screenplay that has been accepted by Fox.*

I, _____, *have total job security.*

HOME

I, _____, *own a rural home with a fireplace.*

I, _____, *have a beautiful yard with healthy trees and flowers.*

I, _____, *own a watchdog that's good with kids.*

I, _____, *have fully covered my house with aluminum siding.*

I, _____, *live in the Westwood district.*

I, _____, *have new Mohawk wall-to-wall carpet.*

I, _____, *employ a maid who cleans my house.*

I, _____, *have an 8-foot Beachcraft hot tub on the deck.*

I, _____, *furnish my home with early-American furniture.*

I, _____, *love spending time at home.*

HEALTH

I, _____, *have full-coverage health insurance.*
I, _____, *feel energetic all the time.*
I, _____, *sleep long and peacefully every night.*
I, _____, *weigh 155 pounds.*
I, _____, *eat every meal without discomfort.*
I, _____, *have a back that is always completely free from pain.*
I, _____, *menstruate on time every month.*
I, _____, *see clearly with healthy eyes.*
I, _____, *have plenty of money to purchase medication.*
I, _____, *have a body totally free of disease.*

FAMILY

I, _____, *can afford necessities for Carol, Tom and Jennifer.*
I, _____, *have children who obey and respect my husband and me.*
I, _____, *get along perfectly with my in-laws, including Mrs. Walsh.*
I, _____, *see a loving look every day in my husband's eyes.*
I, _____, *feel toward my husband like I did fourteen years ago.*
I, _____, *have a wife that is satisfied with me.*
I, _____, *love and admire my wife.*
I, _____, *am a faithful and supportive partner.*
I, _____, *have parents that understand me.*
I, _____, *have sufficient money to send Michael to college.*

RELATIONSHIPS

I, _____, *earn enough money to support Natalie so she doesn't need to work.*

I, _____, *am friends with Jim and Bonnie.*

I, _____, *have a healthy relationship with Andrew.*

I, _____, *attract beneficial people into my life.*

I, _____, *honor all my agreements with others.*

I, _____, *give and receive love unconditionally.*

I, _____, *find it easy to be honest with my room-mate and the people upstairs.*

I, _____, *accept others for who they are.*

I, _____, *satisfy Heather sexually.*

I, _____, *belong to Elite Singles dating service.*

PURPOSE

I, _____, *have money to do whatever I choose.*

I, _____, *know my purpose in life.*

I, _____, *am a member of the North-Shore Seniors club.*

I, _____, *accept responsibility for what happens to me.*

I, _____, *discover something new about myself every day.*

I, _____, *inspire Susan and her friends to help me succeed.*

I, _____, *am enrolled in the Advantage Plus self-improvement seminar.*

I, _____, *always do the will of our Lord Jesus.*

I, _____, *make decisions quickly and easily.*

I, _____, *never stop learning.*

SELF-ESTEEM

I, _____, am as good as or better than anyone.

I, _____, have sufficient money to feel confident.

I, _____, forgive my parents for their behavior.

I, _____, deserve love, success and happiness,
no matter what I do or say.

I, _____, have the motivation and skill to
succeed.

I, _____, look fantastic to Jerry, Nathan, Gail
and those around me.

I, _____, understand myself and love myself.

I, _____, have all the education I need.

I, _____, am a go-getter and great person, with
a strong and powerful personality.

I, _____, earn the respect of everyone I meet.

PROSPERITY

I, _____, know I will always have money.

I, _____, live a life of affluence and abundance.

I, _____, receive a massive influx of energy from
everyone at all times.

I, _____, have a life-style that is extremely fun.

I, _____, grow in wealth with everything I do.

I, _____, am free of debt.

I, _____, have more cash than I know what to
do with.

I, _____, get richer every day just being alive.

I, _____, can hardly keep up with my huge flow
of money.

I, _____, have solved all my money problems
forever.

APPENDIX B
ORGANIZATIONS REFERENCE

THE FOLLOWING IS A LIST of organizations to which you can donate money. The list is intended as a reference when you select places for glad-giving. Feel free to refer to this list if you need to. Otherwise, ignore it.

An effort has been made to keep the list somewhat balanced, representing both sides of issues. I do not personally agree with the viewpoints of every organization listed. Nor do you. Nobody would give money to every group on this list, since many oppose each other. Do not be concerned about the inclusion or omission of any particular organization.

Keep in mind that this list represents only a small fraction of worthwhile organizations. Be sure you consider groups not listed here, such as ones located in your community. Many local groups operate on a small budget and would greatly appreciate anything you give them.

Before you donate money to any organization on this list, I recommend that you first call or write to make certain that they are still operating, that the address is current and that you understand what they do.

Organizations are classified according to primary area of interest. For each organization, you will find the name, year formed, address, phone number and a brief summary statement.

CHARITY

American Red Cross (1881), 17th and D Sts. NW, Washington, DC 20006. (202) 737-8300. Provides assistance for natural disasters.

Salvation Army (1880), 799 Bloomfield Ave., Verona, NJ 07044. (201) 239-0606. Donates to religious and social welfare programs.

National Easter Seal Society (1919), 70 E. Lake Dr., Chicago, IL 60601. (312) 726-6200. Funds assistance for needy and handicapped individuals.

CARE (1945), 600 First Ave., New York, NY 10016. (212) 686-3110. Aid to foreign countries for medical and humanitarian purposes.

Food for the Hungry (1971), P.O. Box E, Scottsdale, AZ 85252. (602) 998-3100. Active in food production and distribution.

Bread for the World (1973), 802 Rhode Island Ave. NE, Washington, DC 20018. (202) 269-0200. Aid to people in third-world countries.

National Food Bank Network (1979). 116 S. Michigan Ave., #4, Chicago, IL 60603. (312) 263-263-2303. Distributes food nationally to charities at the community level.

National Alliance to End Homelessness (1983), 1518 K St. NW, #206, Washington, DC 20005. (202) 638-1526. Working to find solutions to homelessness.

National Coalition for the Homeless (1982), 1621 Connecticut Ave. NW, #400, Washington, DC 20009. (202) 265-2371. Financial assistance for homeless people.

Amnesty International of the USA (1966), 322 Eighth Ave., New York, NY 10001. (212) 807-8400. Human rights advocates supporting political prisoners around the world.

CHILDREN

Save the Children Federation (1932), 54 Wilton Rd., Westport, CT 06880. (203) 221-4000. Supplies help and resources to children in need.

Christian Children's Fund (1938), P.O. Box 26511, Richmond, VA 23261. (804) 756-2700. Sends help to needy children in other countries.

UNICEF (1947), 331 E. 38th St., New York, NY 10016. (212) 326-7000. Supports projects to help children worldwide.

Covenant House (1972), 346 W. 17th St., New York, NY 10011. (212) 727-4000. Assistance and guidance for runaway or homeless children.

Children's Defense Fund (1973), 122 C St. NW, Washington, DC 20001. (202) 628-8787. Actively involved in children's causes.

Child Welfare League of America (1920), 440 1st St. NW, #310, Washington, DC 20001. (202) 638-2952. Provides services for neglected or abandoned children.

Childhelp USA (1959), 15757 N. 78th St., Scottsdale, AZ 85260. (602) 922-4787. Combats child abuse through a national network.

National Committee for the Prevention of Child Abuse (1972), 332 S. Michigan Ave., #1600, Chicago, IL 60604. (312) 663-3520. Promotes public awareness of issues surrounding child abuse.

Big Brothers/Big Sisters of America (1977), 220 Suburban Station Bldg., Philadelphia, PA 19103. (215) 223-5655. Network of volunteers to assist needy children.

Boys Clubs of America (1906), 771 First Ave., New York, NY 10017. (212) 351-5900. Provides educational and vocational help for urban boys.

Girls Clubs of America (1945), 30 E. 33rd St., New York, NY 10016. (212) 689-3700. Provides guidance and education for young girls.

Omega Boys Club of San Francisco (1987), Box 884463, San Francisco, CA 94188. (415) 826-8446. Alternative boys club to promote nonviolence.

Camp Fire Boys and Girls (1910), 4601 Madison Ave., Kansas City, MO 64112. (816) 756-1950. Motivational groups for young children.

Little League Baseball (1939), P.O. Box 3485, Williamsport, PA 17701. (717) 326-1921. Organizes youth baseball.

FAMILY

National Council on Family Relations (1938), 3989 Central Ave. NE, #550, Minneapolis, MN 55421. (612) 781-9331. Devoted to helping marital and family problems.

National Coalition Against Domestic Violence (1978), P.O. Box 34103, Washington, DC 20043. (202) 638-6388. Supplies information and referrals to people in need of counseling.

National Council on Child Abuse and Family Violence (1984), 1155 Connecticut Ave. NW, #300, Washington, DC 20036. (202) 429-6695. Assists victims of domestic violence.

Parents United (1972), P.O. Box 952, San Jose, CA 95108. (408) 453-7616. Provides help for families of abuse.

Parents without Partners (1957), 8087 Colesville Rd., Silver Springs, MD 20910. (301) 588-9354. Support group for single parents.

Roberta Jo Society (1979), Box 916, Circleville, OH 43113. (616) 474-5020. Agency that supplies support to parents of missing children.

Society for Young Victims (1975), 54 Broadway, Newport, RI 02840. (401) 847-5083. Help for families searching for missing children.

National Fatherhood Initiative (1995), 600 Eden Rd., Lancaster, PA 17601. (717) 581-8660. Promotes involvement and responsibility of fathers in rearing children.

Focus on the Family (1977), Colorado Springs, CO 80995. (719) 531-3400. Dedicated to the preservation of the family through teaching Biblical values.

EDUCATION

Association of American Colleges (1915), 1818 R St. NW, Washington, DC 20009. (202) 387-3760. Distributes funds to colleges and universities.

American Council on Education (1918), 1 Dupont Cir., #800, Washington, DC 20036. (202) 939-9300. Promotes higher learning through colleges and universities.

National Education Association (1857), 1201 16th St. NW, Washington, DC 20036. (202) 833-4000. Organization of American educators.

AFS-Intercultural Program (1914), 313 W. 43rd St., New York, NY 10017. (212) 949-4242. Student exchange program for high schools.

Education in a Global Age (1987), 45 St. John St., #1200, New York, NY 10038. (212) 732-8606. Prepares American students for international competition.

Association for Computer Educators (1960), College of Business, James Madison Univ., Harrisburg, VA 22807. (703) 568-6189. Educates teachers and community leaders about computers.

The Algebra Project (1982), 99 Bishop Allen Dr., Cambridge, MA 02139. (617) 491-0200. Promotes understanding of mathematics.

American Library Association (1876), 50 E. Huron St., Chicago, IL 60611. (312) 944-6780. Sponsors improvements in library facilities.

Literacy Volunteers of America (1962), 5795 Widewaters Pkwy., Syracuse, NY 13214. (315) 445-8000. Tutors individuals in reading.

Educators for Social Responsibility (1981), 23 Garden St., Cambridge, MA 02138. (617) 492-1764. Educates students in matters of social responsibility.

Global Education Associates (1973), 475 Riverside Dr., #456, New York, NY 10115. (212) 870-3290. Reports on educational treatment of international issues.

United Negro College Fund (1944), 500 E. 62nd St., New York, NY 10021. (212) 326-1118. Distributes funds to black universities.

HEALTH

AIDS Coalition to Unleash Power (1987), 135 W. 29th St., New York, NY 10001. (212) 564-2437. Coordinates efforts to end the AIDS epidemic.

San Francisco AIDS Foundation (1982), P.O. Box 6182, San Francisco, CA 94101. (415) 864-5855. Education and support for AIDS victims.

Alzheimer's Association (1980), 70 E. Lake St., #600, Chicago, IL 60601. (312) 853-3060. Research and education for Alzheimer's disease.

Muscular Dystrophy Association (1950), 810 Seventh Ave., New York, NY 10019. (212) 586-0808. Research and education for muscular dystrophy.

National Multiple Sclerosis Society (1946), 205 E. 42nd St., New York, NY 10017. (212) 986-3240. Research and education for multiple sclerosis.

American Heart Association (1924), 7320 Greenville Ave., Dallas, TX 75231. (214) 373-6300. Research and education for heart disease.

American Lung Association (1904), 1740 Broadway, New York, NY 10019. (212) 315-8700. Research and education for lung disease.

American Cancer Society (1913), 1599 Clifton Rd. NE, Atlanta, GA 30329. (404) 320-3333. Research and education for cancer.

Leukemia Society of America (1949), 733 Third Ave., New York, NY 10017. (212) 573-8484. Research and education for leukemia.

American Diabetes Association (1940), P.O. Box 25757, Alexandria, VA 22314. (703) 549-1550. Research and education for diabetes.

American Parkinson's Disease Association (1961), 60 Bay St., #401, Staten Island, NY 10301. (212) 981-8001. Research and education for Parkinson's disease.

National Sudden Infant Death Syndrome Foundation (1962), 10500 Little Patuxent Pkwy., #420, Columbia, MD 21044. (301) 964-8000. Research and education for SIDS.

National Society to Prevent Blindness (1908), 500 E. Remington Rd., Schaumburg, IL 60173. (708) 843-2020. Education plus vision and glaucoma testing.

American Public Health Association (1872), 1015 15th St. NW, Washington, DC 20005. (202) 789-5600. Promotes personal and mental health.

National Mental Health Association (1909), 1021 Prince St., Alexandria, VA 22314. (703) 684-7222. Supplies education about mental illness.

DISABLED

National Association of the Physically Handicapped (1958), 440 Lafayette Ave., Cincinnati, OH 45220. (513) 961-8040. Promotes interests of handicapped people.

Information Center for Individuals with Disabilities (1977), 2743 Wormwood St., Boston, MA 02110. (617) 727-5540. Assists the disabled to live independently.

National Federation of the Blind (1940), 1800 Johnson St., Baltimore, MD 21230. (301) 659-9314. Lobbies for equal treatment of blind people.

American Council of the Blind (1961), 1155 15th St. NW, #720, Washington, DC 20005. (202) 393-3666. Distributes information on blindness.

National Association of the Deaf (1880), 814 Thayer Ave., Silver Spring, MD 20910. (301) 587-1788. Lobbies for programs that protect rights of the deaf.

Association for Retarded Citizens (1950), P.O. Box 6109, Arlington, TX 76005. (817) 640-0204. Education regarding mental retardation.

National Stuttering Project (1977), 4601 Irving St., San Francisco, CA 94122. (415) 566-5324. Supplies help to individuals with speech problems.

National Society for Shut-Ins (1970), P.O. Box 1392, Reading, PA 19603. (215) 374-2930. Support for people confined to homes or institutions.

ANIMALS

Fund for Animals (1967), 140 W. 57th St., New York, NY 10019. (212) 246-2096. Activist group promoting animal rights.

American Humane Society (1877), P.O. Box 1266, Denver, CO 80201. (303) 792-9900. Humane treatment of animals.

American Society for the Prevention of Cruelty to Animals (1866), 441 E. 92nd St., New York, NY 10128. (212) 876-7700. Long-standing group involved in general issues of animal welfare.

Animal Protection Institute of America (1968), P.O. Box 22505, Sacramento, CA 95822. (916) 731-5521. Champions the cause of humane treatment for all animals.

Animal Rights Network (1979), 456 Monroe Turnpike, Monroe, CT 06468. (203) 452-0446. Coordinates the animal rights movement.

Animal Welfare Institute (1951), P.O. Box 3650, Georgetown Station, Washington, DC 20007. (202) 337-2332. Active in promoting animal causes.

Friends of Animals (1957), P.O. Box 1244, Norwalk, CT 06856. (203) 866-5223. Promotes pet owner awareness to reduce stray animals.

International Society of Animal Rights (1959), 421 S. State St., Clarks Summit, PA 18411. (717) 586-2200. Works to pass legislation for animal rights.

ENVIRONMENT

Greenpeace USA (1971), 1436 U St. NW, Washington, DC 20009. (202) 462-1177. Stages direct interference against environmental threats.

Sierra Club (1892), 730 Polk St., San Francisco, CA 94109. (415) 776-2211. Promotes environmental study and action.

National Religious Partnership for Environment (1991), 1047 Amsterdam Ave., New York, NY 10025. (212) 316-7441. Religious leaders dedicated to environmental causes.

Physicians for Social Responsibility (1975), 921 SW Morrison, #500, Portland, OR 97205. (503) 274-2720. Education about nuclear war, the national arms race and environmental concerns.

National Wildlife Federation (1936), 1400 16th St. NW, Washington, DC 20036. (202) 797-6800. Resists government destruction of natural resources.

Natural Resources Defense Council (1970), 40 W. 20th St., New York, NY 10011. (212) 727-2700. Drafts and promotes legislation to protect the environment.

Cousteau Society (1978), Box 2002, Grand Central Station, New York, NY 10017. (212) 949-6290. Broad-based education about the environment.

Friends of the Earth (1969), 124 Spear St., San Francisco, CA 94105. (415) 776-2211. Advocates safe, natural and nondestructive life-styles.

National Audubon Society (1905), 950 Third Ave., New York, NY 10022. (212) 832-3200. Conservation of wildlife and natural habitats.

The Nature Conservancy (1917), 1815 N. Lynn St., Arlington, VA 22209. (703) 841-5300. Acquires land to protect threatened habitat.

Wilderness Society (1935), 900 17th St. NW, Washington, DC 20006. (202) 833-2300. Works to preserve public lands.

International Rivers Network (1985), 1847 Berkeley Way, Berkeley, CA 94703. (510) 848-1155. Worldwide preservation of river habitats.

League of Conservation Voters (1970), 1150 Connecticut Ave. NW, #201, Washington, DC 20002. (202) 785-8683. Promotes political candidates who have environmentalist viewpoints.

Worldwatch Institute (1974), 1776 Massachusetts Ave. NW, Washington, DC 20036. (202) 452-1999. Monitors and researches worldwide population and health risks.

Zero Population Growth (1968), 1346 Connecticut Ave. NW, Washington, DC 20036. (202) 332-2200. Dissemination of information about the threat of overpopulation.

Center for Development of Population Activities (1975), 1717 Massachusetts Ave. NW, #202, Washington, DC 20036. (202) 667-1142. Supports population control in developing countries.

POLITICS

American Conservative Union (1964), 38 Ivy St. SE, Washington, DC 20003. (202) 546-6555. Education about political and media issues.

National War Tax Resistance Committee (1982), P.O. Box 774, Monroe, ME 04951. (207) 525-7774. Education about resisting taxes spent on war and military.

Christian Coalition (1988), 227 Massachusetts Ave., NE, Washington DC 20002. (202) 547-3600. Active Christians devoted to conservative causes.

American Civil Liberties Union (1920), 132 W. 43rd St., New York, NY 10036. (212) 944-9800. Protects constitutional rights of individuals and groups.

Progress and Freedom Foundation (1993), 1301 K St., Washington, DC 20005. (202) 484-2312. Future-focused conservatives dedicated to patriotism.

Americans for Democratic Action (1947), 1511 K St. NW, #941, Washington, DC 20005. (202) 638-6447. Advocates liberal policies in government.

Eagle Forum (1975), Box 618, Alton, IL 62002. (618) 462-5415. Promotes conservative causes.

Fairness & Accuracy in Reporting (1986), 130 W. 25th St., New York, NY 10001. (212) 633-6700. Watchdog group targeting irresponsible media.

Heritage Foundation (1973), 214 Massachusetts Ave. NE, Washington, DC 20002. (202) 546-4400. Advocates free enterprise and less government involvement.

Project on Government Oversight (1981), 2025 I St. NW, #1117, Washington, DC 20006. (202) 466-5539. Monitors government activity for errors and inaccuracies.

American Security Council (1955), Washington Communications Center, Boston, VA 22713. (703) 547-1776. Educates public and Congress about strong national defense.

Public Citizen (1971), 1600 20th St. NW, Washington, DC 20009. (202) 588-1000. Consumer lobby for safe products and truthful marketing.

National Taxpayers Union (1969), 325 Pennsylvania Ave. SE, Washington, DC 20003. (202) 543-1300. Crusades for less government spending.

National Coalition Against Censorship (1974), 2 W. 64th St., New York, NY 10023. (212) 724-1500. Lobbies against censorship and restrictions on free speech.

John Birch Society (1958), P.O. Box 8040, Appleton, WI 54913. (414) 749-3780. Supports a conservative focus on social and political issues.

Americans United for Separation of Church and State (1947). 1816 Jefferson Pl. NW, Washington, DC 20036. (202) 466-3234. Campaigning to preserve religious liberty.

Common Cause (1970), 2030 M St. NW, Washington, DC 20036. (202) 833-1200. Working t⌒ make government accountable to citizens.

National Organization for Women (1966), 1000 16th St. NW, #700, Washington, DC 20036. (202) 659-0006. Promotes causes for the women's movement.

American Political Science Association (1903), 1527 New Hampshire Ave. NW, Washington, DC 20036. (202) 483-2512. Promotes arts and sciences in government.

Foundation for a Civil Society (1989), 1270 Avenue of the Americas, #609, New York, NY 10020. (212) 332-2890. Promotes democratic culture and civilized values around the world.

Witness for Peace (1983), 110 Maryland Ave. NE, 311, Washington, DC 20002. (202) 544-0781. Works for peace and justice in Latin America.

Kids Voting USA (1992), 398 South Mill Ave., #304, Tempe, AZ 85281. (602) 921-3727. Educates youngsters on the privilege and responsibility of voting.

ABORTION

Alternatives to Abortion International (1971), 1213 S. James Rd., Columbus, OH 43227. (614) 239-9433. Advises women considering abortion.

Planned Parenthood Federation (1916), 810 Seventh Ave., New York, NY 10019. (212) 541-7800. Education about birth control and childbirth.

Birthright, USA (1968), 686 N. Broad St., Woodbury, NJ 08096. (609) 848-1819. Helps women find alternatives to abortion.

National Abortion Rights Action League (1969), 1101 14th St. NW, Washington, DC 20005. (202) 408-4600. Advocacy group for legalized abortion.

American Pro Life Council (1980), 1612 S. Prospect St., Park Ridge, IL 60068. (312) 692-2183. Lobby to outlaw abortion.

National Abortion Federation (1977), 1436 U St. NW, #103, Washington, DC 20009. (202) 667-5881. Unites caregivers to upgrade abortion facilities.

National Right to Life Committee (1973), 419 Seventh Ave. NW, Washington, DC 20004. (202) 626-8800. Advice and counseling to women about alternatives to abortion, such as adoption.

Physicians for Choice (1981), 810 Seventh Ave., New York, NY 10019. (212) 541-7800. Advocates women's right to choose abortion.

GUNS

National Rifle Association (1871), 1600 Rhode Island Ave. NW, Washington, DC 20036. (202) 828-6000. Defends individual rights to own guns.

Handgun Control, Inc. (1974), 1225 Eye St. NW, Washington, DC 20005. (202) 898-0792. Works to pass legislation to control possession of handguns.

Citizens Committee for the Right to Keep and Bear Arms (1971), 12500 NE 10th Pl., Bellevue, WA 98005. (206) 454-4911. Promotes gun rights based on Second Amendment.

Coalition to Stop Gun Violence (1975), 100 Maryland Ave., NE, Washington, DC 20002. (202) 544-7190. Educates lawmakers and the public about legislation and gun violence.

DRUGS/ALCOHOL

Partnership for a Drug-Free America (1986), 666 Third Ave., New York, NY 10017. (212) 922-1560. Education about the prevention of drug abuse.

Drug Policy Foundation (1992), 4455 Connecticut Ave. NW, Washington, DC 20008. (202) 537-3007. Judges, mayors, police chiefs and other community leaders campaigning for drug legalization.

National Parents' Resource Institute for Drug Education (1977), 50 Hurt Plaza, #210, Atlanta, GA 30303. (404) 577-4500. Research and education to assist parents/teachers.

National Organization for the Reform of Marijuana Laws (1970), 2717 M St. NW, Washington, DC 20037. (202) 483-5500. Lobbies for the decriminalization of marijuana.

Families in Action National Drug Information Center (1977), 2296 Henderson Mill Rd., #204, Atlanta, GA 30345. (404) 934-6364. Supplies drug-addiction information for parents and children.

American Anti-Prohibition League (1993), 4017 SE Belmont St., Portland, OR 97214. (503) 235-4524. National effort to eliminate prohibition of controlled substances.

Group Against Smokers' Pollution (1971), P.O. Box 632, College Park, MD 20740. (301) 459-4791. Advocates banning public smoking.

Mothers Against Drunk Driving (1980), 511 E. John Carpenter Fwy., #700, Irving, TX 75062. (214) 744-6233. Attacks drunk driving through legislative efforts and public education.

Students Against Driving Drunk (1981), P.O. Box 800, Marlboro, MA 01752. (508) 481-3568. Educates students about the dangers of drinking and driving.

MISCELLANEOUS

Optimists International (1919), 4494 Lindell Blvd., St. Louis, MO 63108. (314) 371-6000. Promotes a positive outlook throughout the world.

Promise Keepers (1990), 4891 Independence Ave., Wheat Ridge, CO 80034. (303) 421-2800. Evangelical movement for men.

Human Kindness Foundation (1973), Rt. 1, Box 201, Durham, NC. 27705. (919) 942-2540. Encourages kindness in the world, with emphasis on prison-system reform.

Right Livelihood Awards (1990), Box 680, Manzanita, OR 97130. (503) 368-7652. Alternative to the Nobel Prize, promoting people who demonstrate hope.

U.S. Olympic Committee (1950), 57 Park Ave., New York, NY 10016. (212) 221-1996. Organizes Olympic efforts for the United States.

National Safety Council (1913), 444 N. Michigan Ave., Chicago, IL 60611. (312) 527-4800. Offers education about safety and health issues.

The Impact Project (1991), 21 Linwood St., Arlington, MA 02174. (617) 648-0776. Provides counseling and literature for people taking charge of their money and their lives.

International League for Human Rights (1942), 432 Park Ave. South, #1103, New York, NY 10016. (212) 684-1221. Focus on eliminating racial discrimination.

National Investigation Committee on UFOs (1967), 14617 Victory Blvd., #4, Van Nuys, CA 91411. (818) 989-7278. Educates public regarding UFO sightings and information.

Explorers Club (1904), 46 E. 70th St., New York, NY 10021. (212) 628-8383. Encourages scientific exploration in all areas of study.

American Youth Hostels (1934), P.O. Box 37613, Washington, DC 20013. (202) 783-6161. Manages hundreds of hostels in the United States.

Gray Panthers (1970), 1424 16th St. NW, #602, Washington, DC 20036. (202) 387-3111. Politically active group campaigning against age discrimination.

Hemlock Society USA (1980), P.O. Box 11830, Eugene, OR 97440. (503) 342-5748. Promotes rights of terminally-ill patients to choose death.

National Coalition to Abolish the Death Penalty (1976), 1325 G St. NW, Washington, DC. 20005. (202) 347-2411. Campaigning for a national abolition of the death penalty.

Nature Sounds Society (1983), 1000 Oak St., Oakland, CA 04607. (510) 238-3884. Records sounds from nature and encourages people to listen.

North American Network for Shorter Hours of Work (1995), 69 Dover St., #1, Somerville, MA 02144. (617) 628-5558. Promotes less hours for the standard work week.

Association to Abolish the Automobile (1995), Box 1472, Laguna Beach, CA 92652. (714) 497-6602. Working to end society's dependence on cars.

APPENDIX C
ADDITIONAL MATERIALS

THE FOLLOWING ARE a few products you will find helpful in starting and maintaining your practice of the two-prong method.

The Two-Prong Method Personal Power Pack. $9.95 (plus $3.00 shipping/handling). A special folder containing dozens of useful papers, worksheets and flyers.

Your Personal Power Pack includes many items to assist you with both parts of the two-prong method. Everything you need is provided, and all items can be customized for your personal use. Some items that are included are:

- Expanded worksheets for formulating affirmations
- Custom forms for writing affirmations
- Affirmations performance chart
  (deluxe version, enhanced and enlarged)
- Glad-giving worksheets
- Glad-giving record-keeping forms
- Mini-posters to illustrate principles
- Affirmations and glad-giving reference materials
- Additional instructions and guidelines

The Two-Prong Method Quarterly. $14.95 per year (shipping/handling included). The official newsletter of the two-prong method.

This newsletter, published every three months, contains current information on the two-prong method. It has many valuable hints and suggestions, as well as an abundance of personal success stories from around the globe.

If you want to delve into the inner workings of the two-prong method or explore its ramifications in our world, this newsletter is for you. The only source of this information published anywhere, it is the definitive word on the subject. It will keep you abreast of the latest developments. A subscription to *The Two-Prong Method Quarterly* assures that you stay motivated and get the most from your practice of the two-prong method.

The Two-Prong Method Computer Program. $29.95 (plus $4.00 shipping/handling). Software to assist you with the two-prong method. It requires an IBM-compatible personal computer running Microsoft Windows. [IBM, Microsoft and Windows are trademarks of their respective companies.]

This program helps you with all aspects of your practice. Some features include:

- On-screen worksheets to formulate affirmations
- Record keeping for affirmations and glad-giving
- Printouts of performance charts
- Advanced note taking and record keeping
- Calculations to pinpoint glad-giving
- Accounting procedures for glad-giving
- Lists of organizations
- Detailed reporting capability

To purchase any of these items, use the order form in the back of this book. Be sure to enclose full payment with your order.

APPENDIX D
ADDITIONAL RESOURCES

THE FOLLOWING ARE a few resources you may find helpful as you embark upon your new life of success and prosperity. Although the two-prong method is all you need to do, and you are not required to check out any of these additional resources, you may find some of them useful as avenues of further study or as sources of continued support. Know that these places exist for you if you need them.

As of this writing, every group listed here is actively involved in providing services. Conditions do change over time, however. Be sure you call or write any organization you are interested in to make certain their services are still available and the information is current.

Vivation Seminars and Instruction. Associated Vivation Professionals, P.O. Box 2595, Minneapolis, MN 55402. (800) 829-2625.

Vivation, also referred to as "the skill of happiness," is a technique for integrating your feelings and causing creative breakthroughs. This process, as taught by Jim Leonard, is extremely effective at generating strong visualizations and upgrading addictions to preferences. Vivation is the perfect tool to augment and enhance your program of affirmations and glad-giving. Books, tapes, articles, newsletters, weekend seminars and advanced ten-day trainings are available. Individual sessions with a trained Vivation professional can be arranged in numerous cities and localities throughout the United States and the world.

FI Seminars. New Road Map Foundation, P.O. Box 15981, Seattle, WA 98115. (206) 527-5114.

The FI (Financial Independence) seminars are also referred to as "Transforming Your Relationship with Money and Achieving Financial Independence." These seminars, given by Joe Dominguez and Vicki Robin, teach a collection of exceptionally powerful techniques to guide you in relating to money and using it effectively in your life. The concepts stretch your thinking, shatter old monetary misconceptions and force you to reexamine your priorities. The methods they teach are useful, practical and down-to-earth. You can also purchase tape recordings of this seminar.

Deepak Chopra Workshops and Seminars. Quantum Publications, P.O. Box 598, South Lancaster, MA 01561. (800) 858-1808.

Deepak Chopra's simple wisdom and empowering techniques help tremendously as you create a new and affluent life for yourself. His basic instructions combine mental/spiritual teachings with principles of Ayurvedic medicine. Mr. Chopra has many books, audio cassettes and video cassettes available. He also keeps a busy schedule of workshops and seminars at locations around the country.

Anthony Robbins Seminars. Anthony Robbins Foundation, 9191 Towne Centre Dr., #600, San Diego, CA 92122. (800) 554-0619.

Tony Robbins, well-known for his infomercials on national television, has helped thousands of individuals from all walks of life achieve success and contentment. He has many services to select from, including lectures, seminars, individual counseling, business and corporate consultations, personal achievement research, and full-service professional practice-management. Mr. Robbins is also actively involved in numerous social causes, such as youth programs, homelessness, community improvement and prison reform. A wide range of products and services are available.

Game Plan for Success. F.P. Publishing, 16560 Harbor Blvd., Fountain Valley, CA 92508. (800) 800-7707.

Richard G. Nixon teaches the principles set forth by Joe Karbo. These include techniques closely linked to affirmations and creative visualizations. Advice is also given on topics related to self-employment. Available services include seminars, audio tapes, mini-workshops and small-business consultations. A full list of services and products is presented in the newsletter titled *Game Plan for Success.*

Guerilla Marketing Seminars and Instructional Materials. Guerilla Marketing International, 260 Cascade Dr., Mill Valley, CA 94942. (800) 748-6444.

Jay Conrad Levinson, himself a fan of the two-prong method, started his marketing company on a shoestring. Today he is perhaps the most respected and successful authority on matters relating to small-business marketing. In addition to *The Guerilla Marketing Newsletter,* Mr. Levinson publishes a wealth of information in books, tapes and other media. He also continues to give public seminars. The principles outlined in the Guerilla Marketing material are invaluable to anyone embarking on a money-making venture.

Dale Carnegie Trainings. Performance Training Associates, 135 Beaver St., Waltham, MA 02154. (617) 894-2700.

These trainings focus on building confidence, with emphasis on communication, human relations and leadership. A sales training is also available. The techniques help you reprogram your subconscious mind and project a winning image. These powerful twelve-week courses supply the tools to improve all areas of your life. A number of audio tapes can be purchased too.

Ken Keyes Seminars and Workshops. Caring Rapid Center, 1620 Thompson Rd., Coos Bay, OR 97420. (800) 545-7810.

Mr. Keyes teaches methods for upgrading addictions to preferences, focusing on all types of addictions, relating to all aspects of life. Emphasis is placed on cultivating an attitude of acceptance and finding peace within yourself. These ideas are extremely useful when combined with your program of glad-giving. Ken gives lectures and conducts workshops. A sizeable amount of material is available in the form of books and tapes.

Marshall Sylver Seminars. Sylver Enterprises, 4545 W. Reno, #B-2, Las Vegas, NV 89118. (800) 927-6937.

Mr. Sylver's seminars "entertain, energize, educate and enlighten." His inspiring techniques, aimed at your subconscious mind, are great for cultivating a healthy money consciousness. A lively and exciting speaker, Mr. Sylver conducts one of the most "fun" seminars in existence. Shows, books, newsletters and audio/visual training materials are available.

BIBLIOGRAPHY

THIS IS A LIST OF suggested reading. If you want to further explore the ideas presented in this book, I recommend the following publications. Look through this list and select whatever appeals to you.

Chopra, Deepak. *Creating Affluence*. San Rafael, CA: New World Library, 1993.
> Inspirational reading. A tiny book that gets right to the point. Simple yet powerful concepts for manifesting abundance in your life. An important guide for developing a healthy money consciousness.

Nixon, Richard G. *The Lazy Man's Way to Riches*. New York: Penguin, 1993, 1973.
> Expanded version of the classic Joe Karbo book. Contains specific techniques for visualizing and materializing whatever you want in life. An invaluable source of wisdom and advice.

Dominguez, Joe, and Vicki Robin. *Your Money or Your Life*. New York: Penguin, 1992.

Many detailed and constructive procedures to help you relate to money. A powerful and thought-provoking book. Contains practical methods for honest and purposeful money management.

Peale, Norman Vincent. *The Power of Positive Thinking*. New York: Fawcett Crest, 1952.

A classic. This book serves as an uplifting and motivating confidence builder. Helps eliminate feelings of inferiority. Contains strong religious overtones with plenty of Biblical quotes.

Leonard, Jim. *The Skill of Happiness*. Fond du Lac, WI: Three Blue Herons Publishing, 1996.

Detailed instructions on integrating your feelings and causing creative breakthroughs. Vivation, as taught in this book, contributes not only to prosperity, but to the resolution of all problems and barriers in your life.

Robbins, Anthony. *Awaken the Giant Within*. New York: Fireside, 1991.

Highly motivational. Contains many specific pointers to improve your monetary situation and enhance your experience of life. This book has transformed the lives of many thousands of people.

Hill, Napoleon. *Think and Grow Rich*. New York: Fawcett Crest, 1960, 1938.

One of the most influential books ever written. Valuable background reading for understanding the power of your mind.

Ray, Sondra. *I Deserve Love*. Berkeley, CA: Celestial Arts, 1976.

The definitive work on affirmations. One of the best books ever written on the subject. Includes plenty of helpful suggestions dealing with every conceivable subject.

Keyes, Ken, Jr. *Handbook to Higher Consciousness*. Coos Bay, OR: Love Line, 1975.

Great for understanding the difference between addiction and preference. Contains numerous procedures and suggestions for upgrading an addiction to a preference. Applicable for all types of addiction.

Simonton, Carl O., M.D. *Getting Well Again*. New York: St. Martin's Press, 1978.

Techniques of creative visualization. Although the primary focus of this book is healing serious illness, its message is encouraging and inspirational within all contexts. Many case histories.

Seligman, Martin E.P., Ph.D. *Learned Optimism*. New York: Pocket, 1990.

Honest evaluation of optimism vs. pessimism. Contains techniques to examine your inner dialog and shift your consciousness from that of a pessimist to that of an optimist. Produces astonishing results.

Levinson, Jay Conrad. *Guerrilla Marketing*. New York: Houghton Mifflin, 1993.

A tremendously useful book dealing with marketing. Explores all forms and methods and reveals many secret strategies. Required reading for anyone contemplating a new business enterprise.

Fritz, Robert. *The Path of Least Resistance*. New York: Fawcett Columbine, 1984.
Builds a strong case for the value of acceptance and peaceful living. Discussion of how images lead to reality by means of structural tension. Gives techniques to enhance creativity and achieve what you want. Covers the topic of creativity from conception to result.

Dyer, Dr. Wayne W. *You'll See It When You Believe It*. New York: Avon, 1989.
Emphasizes the power of thought and belief. Gives techniques for setting goals and reaching them. A book capable of producing great personal transformation.

Covey, Stephen R. *The Seven Habits of Highly Effective People*. New York: Fireside, 1990.
Guidelines on living a rewarding and productive life. Based on direct observations of successful people, with emphasis on being proactive rather than reactive.

Wilber, Ken, ed. *The Holographic Paradigm*. Boulder, CO: Shambhala, 1982.
An incredible collection of essays that explore the leading edge of science. This book describes, in detail, the link between energy and matter, thought and reality. Powerful reading material.

Bryant, Dorothy. *The Kin of Ata Are Waiting For You*. New York: Random House, 1971.
A novel. Conveys the message that your thoughts and dreams create your reality and that truth is the most powerful ally you have. Ultimately, you are responsible for the life you imagine—and thus create.

ABOUT
THE
AUTHOR

FOR MORE THAN TWENTY years, Victor Boc has been teaching the techniques presented in this book. By conducting seminars, speaking at universities and writing money-related information, he has helped thousands achieve personal success.

Victor does not let concerns about financial matters dictate how he spends his time. His life stands as a testament to the potency of the methods he teaches. For example...

He was a top-rated radio announcer for fourteen years. In Boston, Denver, Cleveland, New York and the San Francisco Bay area, he served as a telephone-talk-show host, news director and disc-jockey.

He was a professional poker player for eight years. Renowned as one of the world's best, he won at numerous tournaments and played in the World Championship seven years in a row.

He was a nightclub entertainer for five years. Performing to sellout crowds, his energy turned several clubs into lucrative businesses.

Victor has also served as a highly-respected business instructor and consultant. He has operated his own successful business for over twenty-two years.

These days, Victor enjoys writing, editing and computer programming. Living in the hills of central Oregon, he devotes a great deal of time to hiking and romping outdoors. Nearly every day, he and his son play baseball in their yard.

Victor Boc
c/o VORCO PUBLISHING
P.O. Box 5316
Eugene, OR 97405

e-mail: vboc@aol.com

INDEX

To order additional copies of this book or any of the products described in Appendix C, complete the order form on the reverse side of this page. If you are paying by personal check, money order or cashiers check, you must send your order by mail. If you are paying by credit card, you have the additional option of ordering by fax, phone or e-mail.

(Feel free to remove this page from the book.)

ORDER FORM
TWO-PRONG METHOD PRODUCTS

Fill in this form, and then:

📧 for mail orders, send form to: Two-Prong Method Products,
    Vorco Publishing, P.O. Box 5316, Eugene, OR 97405.

📠 for fax orders, fax form to: (541) 485-7424.

💻 for e-mail orders, send information to: twoprong@aol.com.

☎ for phone orders, call toll free: (800) 605-7402.

Name: _____

Address: _____

City: _____ State: _____ Zip: _____

Phone: (____) _____ Fax: (____) _____

Qty	Item	Cost
	Additional copies of this book $12.95 + $3.00 S/H = $15.95 each	
	Personal Power Pack* $9.95 + $3.00 S/H = $12.95 each	
	Two-Prong Method Quarterly* $14.95 per year = $14.95 each	
	Computer Program* $29.95 + $4.00 S/H = $33.95 each	

* For product description, see Appendix C (pg. 265).

Total Payment ⟶
(enclosed in U.S. funds)

❑ Check   ❑ Money Order   ❑ Cashiers Check
❑ Credit Card: ❑ VISA ❑ MasterCard ❑ AMEX

Card number: _____

Name on card: _____ Exp. date: _____

To order additional copies of this book or any of the products described in Appendix C, complete the order form on the reverse side of this page. If you are paying by personal check, money order or cashiers check, you must send your order by mail. If you are paying by credit card, you have the additional option of ordering by fax, phone or e-mail.

(Feel free to remove this page from the book.)

ORDER FORM
TWO-PRONG METHOD PRODUCTS

Fill in this form, and then:

📠 for mail orders, send form to: Two-Prong Method Products, Vorco Publishing, P.O. Box 5316, Eugene, OR 97405.

📠 for fax orders, fax form to: (541) 485-7424.

💻 for e-mail orders, send information to: twoprong@aol.com.

☎ for phone orders, call toll free: (800) 605-7402.

Name: _____

Address: _____

City: _____ State: _____ Zip: _____

Phone: (____) _____ Fax: (____) _____

Qty	Item	Cost
	Additional copies of this book $12.95 + $3.00 S/H = $15.95 each	
	Personal Power Pack* $9.95 + $3.00 S/H = $12.95 each	
	Two-Prong Method Quarterly* $14.95 per year = $14.95 each	
	Computer Program* $29.95 + $4.00 S/H = $33.95 each	

* For product description, see Appendix C (pg. 265).

Total Payment ⟶
(enclosed in U.S. funds)

❏ Check   ❏ Money Order   ❏ Cashiers Check
❏ Credit Card: ❏ VISA ❏ MasterCard ❏ AMEX

Card number: _____

Name on card: _____ Exp. date: _____